W9-CEI-399

Rabbits

SUE FOX

ANIMAL PLANET ♥ PET CARE LIBRARY

Rabbits

Project Team
Editor: Mary E. Grangeia
Technical Editor: Tom Mazorlig
Interior Design: Leah Lococo Ltd. and Stephanie Krautheim
Design Layout: Angela Stanford

TFH Publications®
President/CEO: Glen S. Axelrod
Executive Vice President: Mark E. Johnson
Publisher: Christopher T. Reggio
Production Manager: Kathy Bontz

TFH Publications, Inc.®
One TFH Plaza
Third and Union Avenues
Neptune City, NJ 07753

Discovery Communications, Inc. Book Development Team
Marjorie Kaplan, President and General Manager, Animal Planet Media
Patrick Gates, President, Discovery Commerce
Elizabeth Bakacs, Vice President, Creative and Merchandising
Sue Perez-Jackson, Director, Licensing
Bridget Stoyko, Designer

Exterior design ©2009 Discovery Communications, Inc. Animal Planet, logo and Animusings are trademarks of Discovery Communications, Inc., used under license. All rights reserved. *animalplanet.com*

Interior design, text, and photos ©2006 TFH Publications, Inc.

All rights reserved. No part of this publication may be reproduced, stored, or transmitted in any form, or by any means electronic, mechanical or otherwise, without written permission from TFH Publications, except where permitted by law. Requests for permission or further information should be directed to the above address.

Printed and bound in China
11 12 13 14 15   9 11 13 12 10 8

ISBN 978-0-7938-3765-6

Library of Congress Cataloging-in-Publication Data
Fox, Sue, 1962-
  Rabbits / Sue Fox.
    p. cm. – (Animal Planet pet care library)
  Includes index.
  ISBN 0-7938-3765-0 (alk. paper)
  1. Rabbits. I. Animal Planet (Television network) II. Title. III. Series.
  SF453.F69 2006
  636.932–dc22
                                2006007647

This book has been published with the intent to provide accurate and authoritative information in regard to the subject matter within. While every reasonable precaution has been taken in preparation of this book, the author and publisher expressly disclaim responsibility for any errors, omissions, or adverse effects arising from the use or application of the information contained herein. The techniques and suggestions are used at the reader's discretion and are not to be considered a substitute for veterinary care. If you suspect a medical problem consult your veterinarian.

The Leader in Responsible Animal Care for Over 50 Years!®

www.tfh.com

Table of Contents

Chapter 1

Why I Adore My

Rabbit

Rabbits are some of the cutest animals around. With their long ears, expressive faces, and spry hops, the adorable rabbit is one of the first animals children learn to recognize. They are depicted in modern stories as charming and innocent (*Peter Rabbit*), foolish and conceited (*The Tortoise and the Hare*), or clever and mischievous (*Bugs Bunny*).

The rabbit's breeding ability is legendary, too; hence, the expression "breeding like rabbits." Many ancient cultures revered them as fertility symbols. It is theoretically possible for a single female to produce more than 11 litters a year!

While pet rabbits possess some of these traits—being mischievous and charming with an amazing breeding ability—day to day living with such pets has little in common with how they are portrayed in literature and science.

If you have never kept a pet rabbit, you undoubtedly have expectations as to what it would be like. The best way to have a good experience and avoid disappointment is to know as much as you can about rabbits before sharing your home with one. Knowing ahead of time how they interact with people, the type of care they need, and other noteworthy characteristics, such as their tendency to chew, will help you determine if a bunny can meet your expectations and whether or not you can properly care for one.

As with any pet, the decision to buy one should not be made on impulse. Choosing the right pet requires careful thought and some research. The information in this book will help you make a good choice by answering questions on how well a bunny might fit into your family.

Natural History

Origins

Zoologists originally placed rabbits in the order Rodentia (rodents), which includes animals such as hamsters, guinea pigs, rats, and mice. For various reasons, including the fact that they have two pairs of upper incisors and rodents only have one, rabbits were moved into their own order, called Lagomorpha. This order is divided into two families: Ochotonidae, which includes only pikas, and Leporidae, which includes rabbits and hares.

Hares vs. Rabbits

Hares differ from rabbits because they have precocial young that are born fully furred, with open eyes. Baby hares are able to run within a few minutes of birth. In contrast, most rabbits have altricial young that are born blind, deaf, and furless. Until they develop, baby rabbits are unable to run for several weeks. However, both rabbits and hares have unique skulls that have a joint located at the back of their head, which allows slight movement. This unusual feature helps the skull absorb shock while the rabbit is leaping and running at high speeds.

Rabbits first appeared in recorded human history as early as 1100 B.C., but were not domesticated until the 15th century.

Rabbits are found throughout the world, from the Arctic to the tropics. They live in a variety of habitats, including the arctic tundra, high elevation mountain peaks, pine forests, deserts, open grasslands, and tropical forests. At least 49 species of rabbit are known, with 17 of these living in the United States. Depending on the species, wild rabbits found in North America weigh between 0.5 to 11 pounds (0.23 to 4.98 kg).

Wild rabbits have an interesting array of adaptations. The snowshoe hare (*Lepus americanus*), which lives in regions with snowy winters, molts into a white coat in fall and into a brown coat in spring. This species undergoes striking population cycles every 9-10 years, with huge increases followed by rapidly declining numbers.

Many species of wild rabbit are good swimmers. When pursued by a predator, they will readily enter water and escape by swimming dog-paddle style, with all four feet. The swamp rabbit (*Sylvilagus aquaticus*) of the southeastern United States leads a semi-aquatic life and swims in water to get from one place to another. When hiding from a predator, he may remain submerged except for his nose.

The tiny pygmy rabbit (*Sylvilagus idahoensis*) lives under a canopy of tall sagebrush in the western part of the United States. The only rabbit species found in North America that digs its own burrow, the pygmy rabbit quickly scampers into his underground retreat when eluding a predator. Other species, such as the black-tailed jackrabbit (*Lepus californicus*), live in wide open deserts and rest in shallow scrapes beneath bushes. To escape predators, jackrabbits can hop up to 20 feet (6.1 m) and reach speeds of 30-35

Rabbit History

Seen today in more varieties than ever before, the rabbit has retained its popularity over many centuries. Along with dogs, cats, and mice, rabbits kept as domesticated pets can be traced back as far back as the 1500s.

miles an hour (48.3-56.3 kilometers/hour) over short distances.

Most species of rabbit are solitary. However, the European rabbit (*Oryctolagus cuniculus*) is an exception. This species is social and lives in colonies called warrens, which are a series of dens and tunnels. Dominant males have several females in their territories, and the females establish a dominance hierarchy among themselves. Some groups of rabbit are dominant to others and maintain larger territories.

The European rabbit is the same species as the domesticated pet rabbit. Originally found in Spain, Portugal, and southern France, this single species has been introduced to most countries in the world, including Antarctica, the Australian region, southern South America, and islands off the United States' west coast.

Toward Domestication

The history of the domesticated rabbit is closely tied to human conquest and exploration. About 3,000 years ago, the Phoenicians, an ancient trading people from the eastern part of the Mediterranean Sea, were impressed with the usefulness of the rabbit for meat and fur when they founded new colonies in Spain. Being seafarers, they distributed them to other locations while traveling and trading.

Approximately 2,000 years ago, the European rabbit was introduced to Italy. The Romans kept half-wild rabbits in walled gardens, harvesting them for food and fur. It is likely that this prolific source of food was introduced throughout the Roman Empire. Long-haired rabbits, whose fine hair was spun into yarn, were first recorded during this time. The European rabbit was not found in Great Britain until around 1066 A.D., when it was introduced after the Norman Conquest.

During the Middle Ages, French monks kept rabbits in cages and bred them. Once they began to maintain them in enclosures, the process of domestication truly began. A domesticated animal is selectively bred in captivity by people who control its breeding factors and food supply. Bred for generations to live in close association with people, they differ in many ways from their wild ancestors.

Domesticated rabbits were bred to be docile, predictable, and comfortable around people. In contrast, wild European rabbits have strong natural instincts and will panic when kept in an enclosure. They are afraid of people and will readily bite. Changes in the rabbit's morphology, or body shape, also occurred over time. For example, domesticated rabbits became heavier and meatier than their wild brethren.

Because they were protected from predators, domesticated rabbits with color mutations that normally would have made them conspicuous to a predator in the wild survived and were selectively bred. Thus, they were developed in colors that were not found in nature. By the 1700s, colors such as albino, blue, and yellow were known. All domesticated small animals, including rats, mice, hamsters, rabbits, and guinea pigs, eventually developed mutations from their normal color. Naturally, as pets, a more conspicuous color is not a problem, since they are not subject to predation.

Over time, through additional selective breeding, people created rabbit breeds of different sizes, colors, and types of fur. By the late 19th century, an explosion of different breeds occurred. Some were bred for meat, while others were bred for their attractive looks. New breeds continue to be developed today.

"Meat" breeds also continue to be transported throughout the world. While European explorers and settlers released domesticated rabbits into new lands for food and game, modern transportation has encouraged the establishment of rabbit farms. Because of their rapid growth, fast reproduction, and ability to use forage, rabbits provide a good source of meat for people in developing nations.

Physical Characteristics

Two of the rabbit's most conspicuous features—his long ears and long, jumping hind legs—evolved to help him evade predators. A rabbit can swivel his ears to track the direction of a sound; his keen hearing alerts him to potential danger. Long ears also help a

Spanning centuries of domestication, rabbit breeds of different sizes, colors, and fur types were created through selective breeding.

Common Myths

There are many misconceptions about rabbits and their care. Knowing the facts may help you to be a more responsible and considerate owner:

Myth: Rabbits are easy-to-care-for pets.
Fact: Although rabbits don't need to be walked everyday, they do require daily maintenance: their cage must be cleaned, the litter pan emptied, food and water replenished, and bowls washed.

Myth: Rabbits only live a year or two, so it's a brief commitment.
Fact: Rabbits can live eight to ten years with proper care.

Myth: Rabbits are easy to feed and can exist on rabbit pellets and water.
Fact: Along with pelleted foods, rabbits need hay to maintain healthy digestion, and they also need a variety of fresh vegetables and fruits in their diet.

Myth: Rabbits are outdoor pets.
Fact: Rabbits are social creatures and need to be involved in family activity; they can suffer from loneliness and isolation just as humans do. They thrive nicely as indoor pets.

Myth: Rabbits are dirty and messy animals that smell bad.
Fact: Actually very clean creatures, rabbits bathe themselves quite often throughout the day. They usually try not to soil their bedding, and neither their bodies or droppings have an offensive odor.

rabbit to stay cool by dissipating heat. Those from cold, northern climates have small ears to help conserve heat.

The various breeds of domestic rabbit have a range of ear sizes from small to large, including lop ears that fall to the sides of their head. The domestic rabbit's ears help keep him cool, just as a wild rabbit's ears do. The only sweat glands they have are in their lips, and they are not enough to do the job.

A rabbit's long, jumping hind legs, flexible back, and powerful hindquarters allow for rapid bursts of speed and quick changes in direction. Rabbits that rely on their legs to run usually have long hind legs and live in open areas, whereas those with short legs usually live in brushy areas and bolt underground. The different breeds of domestic rabbit have varying leg lengths, although they obviously do not need to escape predators. For example, dwarfs rabbits have short legs, while the Belgian hare (which is not a true hare) has long, slender legs typical of hares living in vast desert environments.

Unlike rodents, rabbits do not hold food in their front paws. They eat while on the ground, or stand on their hind legs to nibble shrubs. Bulging eyes on the sides of their head provide them with a wide view to detect predators. However, they can't see the area below their mouths and use their whiskers and lips to find plants they like to eat.

Rabbits have six chisel-like incisors in the front of their mouth, two pairs on top and one pair on the bottom. They never stop growing. Their molar teeth also continue to grow throughout their lives. Teeth that continuously grow are termed "open-rooted." Rabbits' teeth can grow up to 5 inches (12.7 cm) per year. The incisors and molars are naturally worn down by chewing on abrasive tough plants. Without continual growth, their teeth would soon wear down and be useless.

Female rabbits are usually larger than males, which is the opposite of most mammals. This trait is present in most breeds of the domestic rabbit. Adult females have a large fold of skin over their throats called the dewlap. Shortly before giving birth, she pulls fur from the dewlap to line her nest.

Behavioral Aspects

Being herbivores, rabbits only eat plants. In the wild, they browse on tender new seedlings and the succulent buds and young leaves of bushes. They eat a variety of foods and select different plant species and plant parts, depending on the time of year. In fall and winter, they usually eat the bark of bushes and trees and nibble grass, while in spring and summer, they eat flowering plants.

Wild rabbits are at the bottom of the food chain, right above the plants they need to eat. Above them are a variety of predators, including coyotes, birds of prey, and snakes. Danger can come from the sky, from behind a bush, or from a burrow in the ground. When alarmed, a rabbit thumps the ground with his hind leg and can also sense ground vibrations caused by the thumps of other nearby rabbits. His first response to danger is to freeze to avoid detection. He then rapidly bolts into a burrow or tries to outrun the predator. If he is caught, he gives a piercing distress call. Rabbits are an important source of food for many predators, but their rapid reproduction helps compensate for their high rate of predation.

Domestic rabbits have a range of ear sizes from small to large, including lop ears that fall to the sides of their head.

Male vs. Female: Gender Issues

A male rabbit is called a buck, and a female rabbit is called a doe. Females can be differentiated from males by a slit-like genital opening that extends toward the anus. In males, the opening is shaped like a point and testicles are present. These differences are difficult to detect in baby rabbits. Consequently, many are incorrectly named. Gender is really only important if you choose to get a second rabbit, in which case you should have your vet make sure sex is accurately determined.

Males and females make equally good pets. Until they become sexually mature, there are no significant differences in behavior or personality. Any differences between them are eliminated if they are neutered or spayed, which tends to eliminate unwelcome reproductive behaviors.

Be aware that a female might be pregnant if she was not separated soon enough from male cagemates. Depending on the breed, females can first breed at around 4 months of age. After a gestation period of 30 to 33 days, baby rabbits are born pink and hairless, with their eyes closed. Litter size depends on breed as well; small breeds produce small litters of 4 to 5 kits, whereas large breeds produce large litters of 8 to 10 kits. Try to buy your rabbit from a source that keeps females separated from males.

Very territorial animals, rabbits have three glands that they use to scent-mark their territory: chin glands, anal glands, and inguinal glands. Dominant rabbits mark much more than subordinate ones. Mother rabbits mark their babies, called kits, with their chin and inguinal glands, which are located in the groin; they will attack any young that smell different from their own. Rabbits use their droppings, which are scent-marked from their anal glands (similar to dogs), to mark their territory by scattering them as they hop around. Pet owners will sometimes notice their rabbit scent-marking by rubbing his chin on table legs or the floor. However, people can't detect the scent this gland produces.

Breeds

Rabbits come with four types of fur. Normal fur is the most common and has two layers—an undercoat and an overcoat. Rex fur is short, stands upright, and feels like velvet. Satin fur is strikingly soft and lustrous. Angora fur is long and fluffy and is used to make clothes. Purebred rabbits are available in dozens of colors and coat patterns. Some breeds have only a few color varieties, such as the Palomino, while others, such as the Netherland Dwarf, are available in more than two dozen color varieties.

Formed in 1910, the American Rabbit Breeder's Association (ARBA) develops the standard for each breed, and they are in charge of the criteria judges use to evaluate rabbits in shows. Rabbit shows are as formal as dog and cat shows. The ARBA currently recognizes 47 breeds of rabbit. Some breeds are old and have been recognized in Europe or in the United States for more than 75 years. Others are new, such as the Mini-Satin White variety, which the ARBA recognized in 2005. It is quite an accomplishment for an individual to develop a new breed as it takes years of devoted hard work.

While dogs differ in temperament based on breed—for example, Pit Bulls are tough fighters and Labrador Retrievers are easy-going—similar stark differences among rabbit breeds do not exist. Any generalizations are typically based on size rather than on breed. For example, dwarf rabbits are excitable and nippy, while large breeds are docile. Plenty of exceptions exist, though. For example, the Dutch rabbit is a small breed and is noted for being calm, whereas the Checkered Giant, one of the giant breeds, is known for being spirited. Moreover, even within a breed, a range of temperaments is found so that some individuals are calm and friendly and others are shy and standoffish.

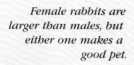

Female rabbits are larger than males, but either one makes a good pet.

If you desire a purebred rabbit, your best approach is to go with a breed whose looks appeal to you; however, coat type and size should be the overriding criteria. Long-haired wool breeds such as the Angora and the Jersey Wooly require a lot of daily grooming. Large rabbits require sizeable cages that take up space, they eat more (and poop more), and they can be heavier to lift and handle if you are not very strong. Within the breed you want, try to find a breeder who breeds for friendly rabbits. Don't overlook mixed breed rabbits. Their only disadvantage is that you are unlikely to know how large they will become as adults.

Is a Rabbit Right for You?

There are two main categories of pet: ornamental and interactive. Ornamental pets include fish and some types of bird. They are enjoyable to watch, and beyond the time spent feeding, cleaning, and monitoring their health, they do not need to interact with

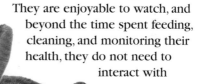

Breed Differences

The different breeds of rabbit are based on size, fur type, color, color pattern, ear type and/or size, and any combination of these features. They have been developed for meat, such as the New Zealand White, which grows quickly and has big muscles; for fur, such as the Angora; and purely for looks, such as the Netherland Dwarf. Size and body type vary widely. Individuals of the giant breeds can weigh up to 20 pounds (9.07 kg), while dwarf breeds weigh less than 3 pounds (1.43 kg).

easy and more pleasant. They can learn the word "no," and some can also learn their name. However, rabbits do require lots of your time. They need daily exercise outside their cage. Kept locked in their enclosure, pet rabbits will become bored and unhappy and eventually develop physical and behavioral problems. Some experts recommend at least three hours of exercise each day. While giving a fixed number is debatable, the fact remains that they must be let out for substantial amounts of daily activity.

Consider whether you have the time (and interest) to do the daily tasks required to care for a rabbit. Besides exercise, you will need to provide your furry pet with two meals a day, as well as clean his litter box and cage every few days. Domestic rabbits are docile and friendly, but you must invest time and patience in order to bond with them. If you lose interest,

their keepers. Ornamental pets are low maintenance. On the other hand, interactive pets are more demanding. They require more than just routine care; they need lots of their keepers' time for play and exercise.

Rabbits are interactive animals. As indoor pets, they can be trained to use a litter box, both inside their cage and when allowed outside to play. This makes caring for them

Social animals, rabbits require more than just routine care; they need lots of their owners' time for play and exercise.

Choose a breed whose looks appeal to you; however, coat type and size should be the overriding criteria.

You could also consider being a "foster parent." Many rescue groups need temporary homes for the rabbits they acquire until permanent situations can be found. Taking in a foster animal means you will provide the same level of care you would if he were your own pet, but only until he has a new home. Besides having the pleasure of doing a good deed (and perhaps even adopting one of your foster wards), you'll also have flexibility should your lifestyle change. The knowledgeable people at most rescue groups can answer any questions that arise and provide support for you in this endeavor.

Rabbits As Pets

Imagine an adorable rabbit that sits up on his haunches and waits, nose twitching, for you to let him out to play. Once he's out of his cage, your rabbit does a bunny dance, twisting and leaping happily in mid-air. Then he's off, investigating his "play room." Some time later, he comes and finds you, nudges you with his nose for some petting, and then he's off again, looking for new adventures. After awhile, he returns and sits next to you while you read a book or watch television. Pet rabbits engage in a number of endearing behaviors. They might lick your hand or, more rarely, groom your hair. Some rabbits will follow their owners around the house, getting underfoot. Many enjoy playing with toys, and a few will even play catch.

your once-friendly pet might become shy, withdrawn, more easily frightened, and less likely to enjoy your company. In turn, you are less likely to enjoy your rabbit. If you are away from home during the day and most of the early evening, consider choosing a different pet that does not require as much daily interaction.

Rabbits have a long life span compared to many other small animals—7-10 years. If you have any doubts about making such a long-term commitment, you could consider adopting an older rabbit from one of the many rabbit rescue organizations. You would provide a good home and some love for a homeless animal.

Why I Adore My Rabbit

However, not all rabbits are affectionate and playful. Many an owner has complained his or her bunny sits in the cage like a lump of fur, or that he is timid and runs away when let out to play. Some rabbits

Adult Weight of Bucks and Does Per ARBA Standards

Breed Types	Weight (pounds)		Breed Types	Weight (pounds)	
	Bucks	Does		Bucks	Does
Small Breeds			Rex	7½-9½	8-10½
American Fuzzy Lop	< 4	< 4	Rhinelander	6½-9½	7 - 10
Britannia Petite	< 2 ½	< 2 ½	Satin Angora	6½-9½	6½-9½
Dutch	3½-5½	3½-5½	Silver Marten	6 – 8 ½	7 - 9 ½
Dwarf Hotot	3 (max)	3 (max)	Standard Chinchilla	5–7	5½-7½
Florida White	4 - 6	4 - 6			
Havana	4½-6½	5¼-5½	**Large Breeds**		
Himalayan	2½-4½	2½-4½	American	9 – 11	10 -12
Holland Lop	< 4	< 4	American Chinchilla	9 – 11	10 - 12
Jersey Wooly	< 3 ½	< 3 ½	Beveren	8 – 11	9 - 12
Mini Lop	4½-6½	4½-6½	Blanc de Hotot	8 – 10	9 - 11
Mini Rex	3-4½	3¼-4½	Californian	8 – 10	8½-10½
Mini Satin	3¼-4¾	3¼-4¾	Champagne D'Argent	9 – 11	9½ - 12
Netherland Dwarf	< 2 ½	< 2 ½	Cinnamon	8½-10½	9 - 11
Polish	3 ½	3 ½	Crème D'Argent	8 – 10 ½	8½ - 11
Silver	4 – 7	4 - 7	English Lop	> 9	> 10
Tan	4 – 5½	4 – 6	Giant Angora	> 9 ½	> 10
Thrianta	4 – 6	4 – 6	New Zealand	9 – 11	10 - 12
			Palomino	< 9	< 9 ½
Medium Breeds			Satin	8½ - 10 ½	9 - 11
American Sable	7 – 9	8 - 10	Silver Fox	9 – 11	10 - 12
Belgian Hare	6 – 9½	6 – 9½			
English Angora	5 – 7	5¾-6½	**Giant Breeds**		
English Spot	5 – 8	5 - 8	Checkered Giant	11 (min)	12 (min)
French Angora	7½-10½	7½-10½	Flemish Giant	> 13	> 14
Harlequin	6½ - 9	7 – 9½	French Lop	> 10 ½	> 11
Lilac	5½-7½	6 - 8	Giant Chinchilla	12 – 15	13 - 16

Select a rabbit that will match your family's personality and lifestyle, like the independent and energetic Checkered Giant—perfect for a busy family.

become territorial and will bite when a hand is placed inside their cage. Regrettably, many of these problems develop due to the owner's misunderstanding of what the pet requires, and sometimes the behavior is due to neglect.

A rabbit's potential pet quality depends strongly on his innate temperament and on the care and attention you provide. Domestic rabbits are instinctively timid and easily frightened; they retain their character as prey animals for which danger is always present. No matter how affectionate, your rabbit will never get rid of his urge to run when scared. Failure to act goes against his instincts to protect himself from being eaten (theoretically, in the case of a pet, of course).

Experts tend to agree that rabbits do not make good pets for young children. Although they may dream of holding and cuddling their bunnies, and photographs showing snuggling bunnies suggest that they, too, also enjoy this activity, rabbits usually don't like being picked up, carried around, or held on a lap for very long. They will tolerate such interactions temporarily,

but will then quickly demand to be put back down. When restrained too long or roughly handled, a rabbit can bite, kick with his strong hind legs, or scratch with his sharp nails. A child that is painfully bitten or scratched is likely to drop the rabbit, which can result in the animal incurring a spinal injury or a fractured or broken leg.

Parents should expect to be the primary caretakers of a young child's rabbit and must show him or her how to properly interact with any pet. Because youngsters occasionally tease animals, they must be watched while playing with them. They can sit quietly on the ground and let the exploring rabbit come to them to say hi. Petting a

Life Span

One of the main differences between rabbits and other small furry pets, such as hamsters and rats, is their life span. Rabbits live a long time—between 7 to 10 years, compared to only 2 to 3 years for hamsters and rats. While many people find long-term care of a rabbit rewarding, others are unable to maintain their interest. If you have any doubts regarding your ability to commit to care long after the novelty is gone, you should seriously consider getting a pet with a shorter life span.

friendly bunny between his eyes, from his nose to his ears, as well as gently petting his jowls, is a sure way to win his friendship.

It is often assumed that small rabbit breeds, such as dwarfs, are more manageable pets for children. However, the opposite is often true since small rabbits can be more skittish and jumpy. If a dwarf rabbit does not want to be held, he can easily jump out of a child's arms, or his struggles will

FAMILY-FRIENDLY TIP

Not for Preschoolers

The decision to make a rabbit a family pet must be carefully considered. Although rabbits are social animals, they tend to be sensitive and timid, and, generally, are not meant to be lap pets. As preschoolers find it hard to differentiate between make-believe and reality, it becomes challenging to assure that the rabbit is not seen as a toy and that his needs and feelings are respected. With several caveats, experts tend to agree that they do not make good pets for very young children, who can have unrealistic expectations and become frustrated (along with their parents) when the animal does not behave as desired.

cause the child to drop him, a situation best avoided. Medium to large breed rabbits are generally recommended for children since they are more docile. However, their size makes lifting and holding them difficult for kids. They must learn to open the cage and let the rabbit come to them rather than trying to pull him out of his home.

Because children do not have long attention spans, caring for their pets can become one more chore unenthusiastically carried out once the novelty wears off. If your child is going to soon become more involved in after-school activities, then a long-lived rabbit that may sit neglected is a poor choice. A better selection might be a hamster or rat, which both have much shorter life spans.

Choosing a Healthy Rabbit

It is always important to select a healthy animal that will be able to give you and your family a good start to years of mutual enjoyment. Never choose a sick animal because you feel sorry for him, because you will both likely be at a disadvantage. No matter where you purchase your rabbit, carefully examine your choice for signs of poor health. The eyes should be clear and bright, with no crusty matter in the corners, or wet, stained fur due to tears. The nose should also be clean of any secretions. Just as some people may wipe their noses on their sleeves, sick rabbits will wipe their noses on their arms. Look at the inside of the front feet and check to be sure the fur

18

Rabbits

in these areas is not wet or matted.

A healthy rabbit should have dense, shiny fur that is not matted or stained. The coat should not show bald areas, excess dandruff, or patches of red skin. You can check by running your hand against the direction of the fur. Evidence of flea droppings, which look like black specks but turn red in water, is an indication that the rabbit has not received good care. Look inside his ears and be sure they are clean and do not emit noxious smells.

The seller should pull back the rabbit's lips and show you that the front teeth are properly aligned. Inspecting them before purchase can help to detect misalignment, a condition called malocclusion that will require veterinary treatment. However, be aware that hereditary malocclusion is often not

Before purchasing your rabbit, carefully examine your choice for good health and ask the seller lots of questions.

detectable in young rabbits. Even if the teeth appear normal at first, changes occur that make the condition more likely as the rabbit grows. Some breeds of rabbit with shortened facial bones, such as dwarfs, are more likely to have hereditary malocclusion.

If the rabbit is calm enough, it can't hurt to listen to the side of his chest to be sure he has no rattling breathing sounds, which may indicate a respiratory illness. When you hold the rabbit, he

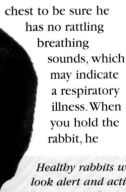

Why I Adore My Rabbit

Healthy rabbits will look alert and active. Their eyes and ears should be clean, and their coats smooth and shiny.

should feel robust and solid, not bony or frail. When he moves, he should not limp or appear awkward.

Choose your rabbit from a clean, uncrowded cage. Rabbits that come from a dirty, crowded environment are less likely to make good pets and are more likely to be unhealthy. The cage should not be grimy or have offensive smells. Unless they are recently weaned, males and females should be housed in separate cages. If juveniles are kept together and their genders have been incorrectly identified, there is a good possibility that a female could be pregnant.

Personality Profile

Be sure to choose a rabbit that has a temperament that will fit your personality and your family's lifestyle. If you want a bunny that will sit quietly on your lap, don't choose a high-energy breed. Likewise, if your bunny will have limited out-of cage time, choose a breed known for its docile temperament and social behavior so that getting less attention won't create stress-related behaviors.

Do not choose a rabbit that is listless or has runny eyes or a runny nose, a rough or thin coat, lumps, or scabs. Dirty, matted fur near the tail could be a sign of diarrhea. Never bring home an animal with obvious symptoms of illness, no matter how sorry you feel for him or how cute he is. Also, do not buy a rabbit that is housed with or near another sick-looking one. It is likely he has been exposed and might also become ill.

More Than One?

Rabbits are social animals and, when properly introduced, enjoy each other's company. Two rabbits will groom each other and will play and rest together. However, if you have never had a rabbit, it is probably best to keep just one. Get to see what keeping a pet rabbit is like before deciding to obtain another one. A second rabbit will require either another cage, or your two rabbits must be housed in a correspondingly larger cage. Don't forget, two rabbits will take more time and work to care for.

It is recommended that you get more than one rabbit if you plan to keep your pets outside in a hutch. Because outdoor rabbits tend to have less interaction with their owners, they need the additional companionship. Two males or two females can be kept together. As babies, most rabbits will get along. But once they reach sexual maturity, they are likely to fight, which can become serious and result in wounds that require expensive veterinary care. Problems can be reduced if the rabbits

knowledgeable, professional individuals.

Where to Buy Your Rabbit

You can buy a rabbit from breeders, pet stores, animal shelters/rescue groups, or through an advertisement in the paper. No matter where you buy your pet, consider asking for a health guarantee that the animal can be returned within 48 hours of sale if he is deemed unhealthy by your veterinarian (information on selecting a vet is provided in Chapter 5). Although a visit to the veterinarian is an additional expense, taking your new pet in for a thorough

21

are altered. Methods to use when housing rabbits who have not been raised together are discussed in Chapter 5.

If you decide to keep a male and female together, you can expect your female to constantly have babies unless she is altered. The reproductive life of a rabbit depends on its breed, but it is about 5-6 years for a buck and 3 years for a doe. Consider whether you will be able to find homes for all the babies born. Pet stores might be interested, but they might not always need them when you are ready to find new owners for your weaned bunnies. Because there are so many rescued animals in need of homes, it is best if you leave breeding to

The Expert Knows

How Old?

A young rabbit tames more quickly and makes a better pet than an older one that has been infrequently handled. Baby rabbits are usually weaned from their mother when they are between four to six weeks old. The earliest age to purchase a baby rabbit is eight to ten weeks of age. Do not buy one that was just weaned. Going to a new home is a stressful event that can cause him to get sick. A slightly older baby bunny will be hardier and just as cute.

Rabbit ownership comes with many responsibilities. Be sure you can make a commitment for the lifetime of your pet before bringing him home.

checkup can help avoid a potentially larger expense or heartbreak down the road. The vet can also confirm whether the rabbit is a female or a male.

Breeders

You can locate breeders of purebred rabbits through the American Rabbit Breeder's Association (their address is located in the resources section at the back of the book). Breeders typically specialize in one or more breeds of rabbit. Some have large operations housed in commercial barns, while others are small-scale and raise rabbits in their homes. Either way, your best choice is someone who selectively breeds for friendly animals and who regularly handles the babies so they are already used to people. A good breeder should ask you questions to make sure you are properly prepared to take care of a rabbit.

Many breeders affiliated with ARBA compete in rabbit shows. Youngsters involved in 4-H and Future Farmers of America clubs also breed and show purebred rabbits. Local groups can be contacted through agriculture extension offices. If you want to get involved in showing, you should obtain a show-quality rabbit. Expect to pay more for a purebred show-quality rabbit compared to a purebred pet-quality rabbit. It should be noted that there is nothing wrong with a pet-quality rabbit. He might have incorrect color or other features that would make it difficult to compete successfully in shows. However, these show faults do not affect the rabbit's appeal or his ability to live a long, happy life as a pet.

Pet Stores

Pet stores are convenient and most full-line stores sell rabbits. Some carry only purebred rabbits, while others might also sell mixed breeds. If you live in an area with numerous pet stores, shop around. Choose a pet store that is clean, and one where the staff has specific knowledge of rabbits and can help you purchase the necessary supplies. Try to go to the store when it is not busy so you can take your time while you evaluate the rabbit's health and personality.

Animal Shelters/Rescue Groups

Animal shelters and humane societies often have rabbits available. These animals have usually been turned in because their owners no longer want them. The rabbits available at shelters are likely to include a variety of ages and breeds, as well as mixed breeds. Shelters do not always have them available for adoption; however, rescue groups almost always do.

Rescue groups obtain rabbits from various sources: shelters, animal control agencies, rabbits found abandoned, and occasionally from individuals. The House Rabbit Society is a well-known rescue group. It is a nationwide volunteer organization with local chapters that foster these animals so they are not euthanized. If homes

cannot be found, members commit to providing them permanent places in which to live out their natural lives. All rabbits are given necessary medical care, including spaying or neutering.

Rescue groups have an application process to carefully screen potential adopters. Their members put a lot of time, care, and money into each animal and want to make sure he will be provided with a good, permanent home. They will help to match you with the best fit in terms of rabbit personality. The volunteers are knowledgeable and can answer any questions that arise later. As with

If You Adopt...

Expect to be thoroughly questioned by a rescue volunteer if you apply to adopt a foster rabbit. These people are professionals and experts who want to be sure they place their animals in the right homes. They also want to assure that you are making a long-term commitment in order to avoid putting the bunny through another traumatic upheaval in his life. This process works both to your advantage and his.

animal shelters, a variety of rabbits are likely to be available for adoption. There is a fee, but it is much less than you would pay to buy one from a pet store or breeder, and then have a veterinarian spay or neuter your pet. If, for some reason, your choice does not work out, the group usually requests you return the animal to them.

Newspapers

If you check the pet section of a newspaper, you might see an advertisement for a "rabbit with cage and supplies." Usually, the rabbit is an adult, and he and his supplies are offered at a low price because the seller just wants to be rid of him. He might need a new home because of divorce, a family move, lack of time, or lack of interest. Do be cautious. You don't want a rabbit that has been ill-treated or neglected, because he is likely to be unfriendly and might even be mean. The person selling him should be able to take him out of his cage and handle

him without being bitten, kicked, or scratched. Once out of his cage, the rabbit should be calm, not frightened and skittish. While he might have a charming character just waiting to blossom, most beginning owners lack the expertise to help a mean rabbit become a good pet.

When selecting your rabbit, carefully observe his temperament and behavior to ensure you will have a friendly, adaptable pet.

Your Rabbit's Personality

An animal's temperament, or personality, is important to the quality of your pet owning experience. There is a large variation in rabbit temperaments. Friendly rabbits are curious and will come up to people and seek attention. They love to be petted and will nudge you with their nose for more. If given the opportunity, they will follow you around, and some even seem to want to be picked up. Outgoing rabbits often sleep confidently on top of their nest box and are not bothered by household noises and events. In contrast, shy ones might flinch when touched or consistently move away from your hand. They appear uncomfortable and spend considerable time inside their nest boxes.

Just like cats, a shy rabbit can be encouraged to be less shy, but he will never be as easygoing as a naturally friendly individual. Most pet owners enjoy a confident, bold pet better than they do a shy and skittish one. Besides the obvious advice to avoid a rabbit that is aggressive and tries to bite, scratches or struggles frantically when held, or runs away from your hand, how can you find a rabbit with a more friendly character?

No matter where you purchase your rabbit, spend at least 30 minutes getting to know your choice before deciding whether or not to bring him home. In an enclosed, relatively quiet space, allow the rabbit time to explore his new surroundings; any sounds or actions you make during the first 15 minutes that cause a reaction are not very indicative of his character. He will be spending that time thoroughly investigating and marking his territory. After he has finished, a friendly rabbit will be curious and come up to you for petting, whereas a shy rabbit will run away from your offered hand, no matter how gently you talk to him. Naturally, there are rabbits with in-between personalities that might initially be afraid, but will eventually be inquisitive and sniff your hand.

Of course, other factors will also affect your rabbit's personality, such as the environment you provide and how often you play with him. But you can at least increase the likelihood that you are buying a rabbit whose temperament may more closely match what you desire.

Altering

Altered rabbits make better pets because they are calmer and more people-oriented. They are less territorial, and their instinct to spray urine is eliminated. Odors from a rabbit's droppings and urine are reduced due to less hormone production. Litter box "accidents" tend to be less frequent. Finally, altered rabbits are more likely to get along and fight less with other rabbits. While not all undesirable behaviors will be gone, they are likely to be greatly diminished.

25

Why I Adore My Rabbit

Spaying or neutering your rabbit can help prevent diseases and reduce undesirable behaviors.

Keep in mind that the personality of an adult rabbit is likely to be more "fixed" than that of a baby rabbit. If the animal you want is young and exhibits shyness, you may be able to socialize him to be friendlier with training.

Why Spay or Neuter?

Spaying and neutering (also called altering) a rabbit used to be an uncommon procedure. As the popularity of having them as pets grew, a better appreciation and understanding of their potential as companion animals led to an increased awareness of the procedure's benefits.

Just as kittens and puppies grow up, so too will an adorable baby bunny. Once sexual maturity is reached, behavior often changes—the rabbit will develop behaviors aimed at finding a mate and breeding. Owners usually do not appreciate these changes, many of which are undesirable for a house pet.

Male rabbits spray pungent urine to mark their territories, a most unwelcome behavior in a house. Adult males can sometimes become aggressive, display excessive mounting behavior, and be more difficult to handle. Female rabbits may undergo false pregnancy and even pull hair and make a nest in the expectation of giving birth. They may also spray urine and be aggressive, not to mention the possibility of becoming pregnant if a male is around. Rabbits of either sex may stop using their litter boxes.

These reproductive behaviors lead to problems that cause some pet owners to give up their rabbits. Surgically altering them so they can no longer breed is highly recommended as doing so typically eliminates or reduces undesirable behavior. Spaying female rabbits is also recommended as a means of preventing disease, specifically uterine cancer, which is relatively common in females older than two years of age. Because altered rabbits are less prone to reproductive diseases, they tend to live longer than those that are not spayed or neutered.

Females mature earlier than males. Males do not reach maturity until more than one to two months after puberty. The best age to alter a rabbit is shortly after sexual maturity. This varies according to breed. Small rabbit breeds develop rapidly and are mature at 4 to 5 months of age. Breeds of medium size reach maturity at 4 to 6 months. Large breeds are mature when they are between 5 to 8 months.

With all the benefits ascribed to spaying or neutering, many people still do not opt for the procedure because it is an additional expense that they are reluctant to pay for or cannot afford. The actual cost varies depending on where you live. Although it is expensive, the benefits are significant enough that you are strongly urged to budget for the operation, or you can get pet insurance. Doing so will eliminate many of the problem behaviors that cause rabbit owners to abandon their pets at shelters each year.

When You Can't Keep Your Rabbit

For various reasons, some people are unable to provide a "forever home" for their pet. If you can't keep your rabbit, you should try to find him a new home by asking friends or your veterinarian if they know someone who may want to adopt him. Also try advertising in the paper. If that does not work, you should relinquish your rabbit to a humane society or shelter. Do not release him into the wild in the mistaken belief that he will have a better chance at a happy life. He will most likely be eaten by a predator such as a coyote, killed by a car, or slowly die from an illness. The following organizations will accept rabbits and work to find them new homes:

Friends of Rabbits
information@
friendsofrabbits.org

House Rabbit Society
(510) 970-7575
care@rabbit.org

Rabbit Welfare Association
England
44-08700-465249
www.houserabbit.co.uk/

The Stuff of
Everyday Life

Now that you have decided on which rabbit to purchase, you are surely anxious to bring your new pet home. Before doing so, however, it is important that you have everything ready for him when he arrives so that he can immediately feel comfortable and secure. You will want to make his homecoming pleasant and be able to provide for all of his needs.

Your rabbit's cage is the most expensive piece of equipment you will need to buy. Luckily, a cage is a one-time expense that should last for the lifetime of your pet. The type of enclosure you need depends on where your bunny will live. Rabbits can be kept indoors in cages or outside in hutches.

Some fanciers are adamant that pet rabbits should only be kept indoors as "house rabbits." They believe that the type of bond you form with an animal kept in your home is different from one that is kept outdoors. For example, a house rabbit can be taken out of his cage in the evening after school or work. You can visit with him while relaxing, watching television, or reading a book. When kept inside, he has the opportunity to express his personality in a way not possible when he is kept outdoors. In turn, you will develop a more enjoyable relationship with your rabbit because you will spend more time with him.

There are other good reasons to keep your rabbit indoors. He will be safer, and because he is kept in the home as a family member, he is less likely to be neglected. While an outdoor rabbit is still enjoyable, the time you have to interact with him is limited to daylight hours. Unpleasant weather also reduces the amount of time he can spend playing outside his hutch and the opportunities you are likely to have visiting with him. But with a commitment to his care and company, he can still be a fun pet.

Indoor Housing

Types of Cage

Cages are available in many shapes, sizes, and styles. Indoor rabbit cages are usually made of galvanized steel, with a metal or plastic tray. Some trays are attractively colored and can be coordinated to match a room's décor. They either slide out for quick cleaning or snap off.

Because rabbits are not natural climbers, a cage that provides maximum floor space rather than vertical height is best. Although they might look spacious and fun, the large two- and three-story cages sold for ferrets are not recommended.

Planning Ahead

Before you bring your rabbit home, you'll need to have a few supplies on hand to make him feel safe and comfortable when he arrives. The better prepared you are, the smoother the transition will be for your already anxious rabbit, who will need time to adjust to his new surroundings and family. Having everything in place will make him feel welcome and secure.

The cage you purchase should be large enough to accommodate your rabbit, his nest box, food bowls, water bottle, and toys.

However, rabbits do enjoy surveying their domain from an elevated lookout, and some enclosures provide raised platform shelves just for this purpose.

Most manufacturers label their cages for specific kinds of small pets. By choosing a cage designed for rabbits, you can assume the size of the wire, called the gauge, is suitable and that the spaces between the wire mesh are not too large or too small. No matter what, the wire mesh that composes the body of the cage should feel strong and durable, not soft and flimsy.

Regardless of what style you choose, a few general rules apply. Being able to comfortably reach all areas within the cage to perform daily tasks such as cleaning the litter box and supplying fresh food will help make these chores much easier. Whether a cage has both a top and front door, or one large front

door, at least one opening should be large enough for you to be able to remove your rabbit without effort. Check that there are no sharp metal edges on the doors and that they latch securely and cannot be easily pushed out at a corner by a persistent rabbit.

Because a rabbit's cage is large to move, one or more handles can make transporting it easier. Do not keep your rabbit in a glass or plastic aquarium. This type of housing does not provide sufficient ventilation and can allow heat and ammonia to build up to dangerous levels.

Cage Floor

Rabbit cages have three types of floors: wire mesh, slat, or solid. All three styles are suitable, with a few caveats. Wire floors are designed to allow droppings and urine to fall below the

New Home Jitters

When you first bring your rabbit home, he might be nervous. Let him settle down and get used to his new surroundings before playing with him. Use this time to think of a name for him, which will help you tame him. He will learn to associate it with feeding and play time. In many cases, a rabbit is immediately comfortable in his new home and will respond well to your friendly attempts. You can offer him some food in your hand, but if he seems shy and skittish, leave him alone for awhile or just talk soothingly to him.

mesh so the rabbit stays clean and dry. This design predates the use of litter boxes. Now that they are commonly available for rabbits, this feature is no longer necessary. However, it is useful while your rabbit is learning to use his litter box.

Rabbits have tender feet. Those housed on exposed wire floors may develop sore feet, a condition called ulcerative pododermatitis. This can be prevented by providing an area of solid floor large enough for your rabbit to comfortably sit on. You can use a piece of untreated wood or cardboard. Your rabbit will chew both of these items, so they will need to be replaced occasionally, particularly the cardboard. In summer, your rabbit will appreciate a cool piece of tile.

Cages with a slat bottom were designed to alleviate sore feet and are more comfortable. However, it's still a good idea to provide a piece of solid flooring. The spaces between the slats will allow any excrement to drop below your rabbit's living space. Solid floor cages are designed for use with a litter box. Because rabbits produce a lot of urine and droppings, it is unsanitary to house them without providing one.

Cage Size

The minimum size enclosure to consider is 3 feet (0.9 m) long, 2 feet (0.6 m) wide, and 18 inches (0.5 m) high. Even a dwarf rabbit needs an enclosure this size. Larger breeds need an even bigger enclosure. Remember to buy a cage for your rabbit's adult size, not his baby size. If he is a mixed breed and you don't know how large he will get, always err on the side of the largest one you can afford.

The cage you choose must be a comfortable, roomy home for your pet. It should have enough space for a litter box, eating area, nest box, and still provide hopping room. Ideally, your rabbit should be able to move at least three hops along the enclosure's length without running into any cage furniture, and he should be able to stand up on his hind legs without his ears touching the top of it—this is where he'll spend most of his day.

Litter Boxes

Litter boxes made specifically for small animals such as rabbits and ferrets are sold at pet stores. They are similar to those for cats, or they are triangular in shape and fit in a cage corner. Most are made of plastic, but some are constructed of metal and wire mesh. The litter box you select should be large enough for your adult rabbit to comfortably sit and turn around in. For this reason, corner litter boxes, which tend to be small, work best for dwarf rabbits. Small animal litter boxes have a low rise in the front that makes it easy for them to enter and leave. If you are unable to find this size and style, you can modify one for cats. The litter box should be placed at one end of the cage, and your rabbit's nest box, food dishes, and water bottle should be placed at the other end. (Information on how to train your rabbit to use his litter box is provided in Chapter 6.)

Litter

An absorbent material is needed in the litter box. You can use wood shavings such as pine, aspen, spruce, or pine treated with chlorophyll for odor control. Bedding products made from recycled paper or wood pulp are designed to help control or eliminate odor; recycled paper does not contain harmful inks, dyes, or significant levels of heavy metals. Since most newspaper inks are now vegetable-based not petroleum-based, they are safe for small animals as well.

While some types of bedding contain odor-masking agents, such as the chlorophyll in shavings, recent innovations have been spurred in part by the quest to control or eliminate odor. Scientifically developed products made from a variety of materials, such as recycled paper, do not just mask odor, they are designed to reduce odor by controlling the formation of ammonia. Such bedding materials promote a healthier environment for rabbits.

Purchase a cage for your rabbit's adult size, not his baby size, as he will outgrow it quickly.

The bottom of the cage floor should be solid to protect your rabbit's tender feet.

Although it has little absorbency, straw is suitable. Other choices include cat litters made from recycled newspaper or compressed sawdust. Corn cob litter is sometimes suggested, but because it does not absorb liquids well or control odors, it is not the best choice. Moreover, if you wait more than a few days between cleanings, you might find mold growing on it. Concern over possible gut impaction from a rabbit eating the litter is another good reason not to use it.

Keep in mind that rabbits will taste, and sometimes eat, whatever is put in their home, including the litter in their litter box. For this reason, clumping cat litters are not recommended. Purposeful or incidental consumption of the litter can lead to a gut impaction and risky, expensive surgery. Experts disagree as to the suitability of regular clay cat litter. As long as it is dust-free and unscented, some authorities think it is suitable for rabbits. Others caution against it due to the risk of dust irritating the respiratory tract and the rabbit consuming some and being unable to pass it. Because other suitable litters are readily available, it is probably best to avoid clay litters.

Some owners use alfalfa pellets. While they work fine, they are not recommended. Adult rabbits should be fed a known quantity of pellets to prevent obesity, and snacking from the litter box can increase your pet's calories.

Litters vary in price, absorbency, and odor control. If you use a less absorbent material such as straw, you should expect to change the litter box at least every day. With more absorbent products, cleanings can often be performed every other day. If your rabbit kicks the litter out of the box, try using a deeper one with higher sides.

Bedding

Bedding is used to absorb moisture (from urine, and water from the occasional leaking bottle), reduce odors, and provide a warm, dry environment for your pet. Even though there is a litter box in the cage, the floor should still be covered with some type of bedding. The same types of litter used in the litter box can also be used as bedding on the cage floor. Only a thin layer is necessary in the cage tray beneath a wire floor, just enough to absorb any accidents. The tray can be lined with newspaper only, but this will do little for odor control. If your rabbit is housed directly on the cage floor, place enough bedding in it to cover the smooth floor and to provide traction. The sides of the tray should be high enough to prevent your rabbit from kicking any bedding out.

Bedding and litter are important components of your rabbit's environment, and they can affect his health. Ideally, it should not be dusty as it can irritate the respiratory system or aggravate an existing respiratory ailment. In general, paper pulp and recycled paper products tend to be lower in dust compared to wood shavings.

Nest Boxes

Your rabbit needs a nest box for sleeping and security.

> ### Bigger is Better
>
> Do not buy a small cage on the assumption that your rabbit will always be allowed time outside of it. Lifestyle changes and unanticipated events can temporarily create situations that result in less play time, causing your rabbit to be stuck in an area that is too small. In addition, a cage that is too confining will become dirty and smelly more quickly and can lead to abnormal behaviors. So, buy the biggest one you can afford.

Clean your pet's cage on a regular basis, and dispose of uneaten food and soiled bedding quickly.

The Shavings Controversy

Shavings made from softwoods, which include pine and cedar, are still the most common type of bedding for small pets. They have been popular because they are relatively inexpensive and are often fragrant smelling, particularly cedar shavings. The pleasant smell associated with these materials is due to the aromatic compounds found in wood. However, cedar shavings have been implicated as both causing and aggravating respiratory problems in small animals. Few controlled scientific studies have documented these problems; more common are reports that when a pet was removed from cedar shavings, its symptoms of poor health disappeared (such as breathing distress). A few studies have shown that cedar shavings affect liver function in rats and mice, although the effect is so minute it is only of concern to research scientists. While not all experts agree that cedar shavings pose a risk, it has become common practice to recommend against using them for small pets such as rabbits.

Some hobbyists also argue that pine shavings are harmful. However, there is no scientific evidence supporting this assumption. Research facilities across the country still house small animals on pine shavings. If there were any detrimental effects, scientists would be the first to switch beddings because they cannot afford to have their research animals harmed. If you wish to avoid the issue completely, you can use shavings made from hardwoods such as aspen and spruce. However, they tend to be more expensive than pine and are not available throughout the country.

(Keep in mind that many pet stores do not provide nest boxes for their rabbits to make them easier for you to see. Because they are only in the store for a brief period, no harm is done. However, they should have nest boxes in their permanent homes.) This "bedroom" gives your rabbit a safe hiding place to retreat to away from loud noises and any disturbing activity outside his cage. Unless absolutely necessary, never pull your rabbit out of his nest box. Instead, call to him and let him come on his own terms. His nest box is his refuge.

This "hideaway" should be large enough for your rabbit to comfortably stretch out in, with an opening that allows easy entry. You can buy one made of metal, wood, or plastic at a pet store. The metal ones are the most durable. However, metal also tends to stay cold when it is cold and warm when it is warm. Unless the box is lined with wire mesh, your rabbit will chew it. However, chewing wood helps to keep teeth trim and should not be discouraged. A chewed, unlined wood box will just need to be replaced more often. It is also best to remove a plastic nest box if your pet chews on it to reduce the risk of indigestible pieces being swallowed. Any commercially made nest box should have a large opening for easy cleaning. You can also make a nest box from a cardboard box. Once the box becomes chewed or smelly, you will need to replace it. Place

comfortable nesting material such as straw or pine shavings in it.

Food Dishes

Your rabbit needs two dishes for his food and a hay rack. One dish will hold dry foods, while the other should only be used for moist foods. Choose sturdy ceramic or heavy-duty, durable plastic dishes that can't be easily tipped over. Unless they clip to the side of the cage, a rabbit can easily move a light-weight dish and strew the contents about the floor. Some may chew plastic dishes; if this is the case, switch to a ceramic dish.

Dry foods can also be served in a J-shaped hopper that clips securely to the cage. Hoppers hold large amounts of food and work best for rabbits fed unlimited quantities, such as babies. Be aware that your rabbit might defecate in his food bowl. This is nothing to be concerned about, but you can prevent this behavior

Your rabbit will need two dishes for his food, one for dry foods and another for moist foods. Choose heavy-weight dishes that won't tip over.

by using a dish that your rabbit cannot sit in.

A daily ration of hay should be placed in a hay rack attached to the side of the cage. The rack's height can be slightly above ground level or higher so your rabbit must stretch up to eat. You can place it on the cage floor, but your rabbit will waste some when he tramples on it, and he might also defecate on it. Rabbits do enjoy burrowing and tromping through hay. If you have an inexpensive source of quality hay, you could consider placing it on the floor.

Water Bottles

Provide water in a gravity-flow water bottle commonly sold in pet stores. The sipper tube should be placed at a comfortable height for your rabbit; typically, a bit higher than his head. Do not place the water bottle over a food dish in case of accidental leakage. To prevent leaks, the tip of the bottle should not touch the cage bedding or any cage furniture.

Be sure to buy the largest bottle specifically

Fresh water should be provided daily. It's best to use gravity bottles as water in bowls tends to become easily soiled.

made for rabbits. Choose one with hatch marks (or make your own with an indelible marker) to help you monitor water intake. Rabbits must always have water available. Ideally, you should empty and refill the bottle every day, although most owners fill it every other day.

Toys

While in their cages, rabbits require some form of entertainment or they become bored and depressed. Toys give them something to do and will make them more enjoyable pets. Rabbits enjoy playing with almost anything you put in their cage. Their play can involve chewing, and often the destruction of toys, so make sure you offer safe items.

You can offer your rabbit a hard block of wood to chew, cardboard tunnels, pine cones, and cardboard boxes. He'll even shred a pile of newspapers or chew apart an old phone book. Just be sure that the covers have been removed and that the pages are not covered with a glossy coating. Many wooden toys made for large parrots are safe. Wood chews keep rabbits busy and active, as well as providing a hard surface for them to gnaw, which helps to keep their

Water: Bottles vs. Bowls

It is best not to give your rabbit water in a bowl, not even in a heavy clay crock that will not tip. His normal daily activities will quickly cause it to become dirty. Cage bedding and rabbit droppings will also foul the water. When your rabbit hops around, it will splash, creating a moist environment in which bacteria and mold can thrive. Moreover, rabbits with dewlaps (the large fold of skin beneath the chin) tend to get them wet when they drink. This continual wetting can lead to moist dermatitis and bacterial infection.

teeth in good shape. Tree branches from alder, willow, maple, ash, and apple are also safe; just make sure the trees were not treated with any kind of chemical. Roll-about balls made for hamsters and larger pets such as ferrets should not be used with rabbits. Most rabbits are too large for these toys and become stressed or even panic in a confined space. Moreover, their natural gait is a hop, which is incompatible with the roll-about balls.

The greater the variety of toys, the more fun your rabbit will have, and the more fun he will be to watch. By providing him with lots to play with and explore, you help reduce the likelihood of your pet becoming overweight. Do not overcrowd the cage with toys, however. Alternating them is a trick that dog and cat

owners have used for years, and it can be used by rabbit owners as well. Let your pet play with a toy for a week, then take it away and replace it with a different one, and so on. By continually switching your pet's toys, you keep him active and interested in exploring his environment.

Rabbits require some form of entertainment or they become bored and depressed.

Home Sweet Home

When you first bring home your new rabbit, you might want to keep his cage in a fairly quiet location until he adjusts to his new surroundings. You can then move it to a more active, family-centered location. Alternatively, temporarily covering half of the cage with a cardboard box will increase your rabbit's sense of security and decrease his sense of vulnerability.

Where to Keep the Cage

A rabbit's cage is relatively large, and deciding where to keep it takes some thought. To begin with, do not place it near a heating or air conditioning vent, fireplace, wood stove, drafty window, a door that is constantly opened and closed, or in direct sunlight. Remember that the sun shifts position throughout

Home or Jail Cell?

Just as some humans tend to think of cages as a sort of isolated prison, a rabbit who lives his whole life in a cage may feel the same. However, a rabbit that is allowed ample out-of-cage time will see it more as his private den and refuge. Along with being good for his mental health, the stimulation and exercise are also necessary for his well-being and longevity. Bunnies that are bored and confined will often resort to destructive behavior and could possibly hurt themselves in the process.

the year. Rabbits are very sensitive to high heat, and temperatures above the upper 80s (30°-32°C) can lead to heatstroke. Comfortable temperatures for a rabbit correspond to those found in most homes, between 59°-72°F (15°-22.2°C).

Your rabbit should be part of your family, and his cage should be placed in a location where everyone can enjoy him. Even if he belongs to a child, a family room is often the best location. A bedroom is often not suitable because nighttime feeding noises and hind foot thumping can disturb sleep. Children thrive on attention, and sharing discoveries of their pet's antics with other family members will encourage their long-term interest. Rabbits are also social creatures and can adapt to a family's activities. However, find a balance between your rabbit languishing in a quiet room and being subjected to too much boisterous activity.

The floor is not an ideal location for the cage as it can be too drafty in winter. You can place it on a small table or cinder blocks (sold at lumber stores) covered with an attractive fabric. You can then store supplies under it. Keeping the cage somewhat low to the ground will enable your rabbit to easily exit and enter the cage via the door, which acts as a ramp when he is allowed outside play. Until your rabbit has been safely introduced to other family pets (see Chapter 6), his cage should be placed out of their eye-level view. He will not enjoy a salivating dog or a staring cat outside (or on top of) his refuge.

Daily or Alternate Days

Empty the litter box daily or every other day. Using a kitty litter scoop, remove any droppings or urine-soaked bedding. Wash the dishes every few days; most can be safely cleaned in a dishwasher. Dishes that hold moist foods should be frequently washed to prevent the growth of mold and bacteria. Replace any that are cracked or chipped. Purchasing a second set can make cleaning easier since you can provide food in clean receptacles while others are being washed.

Weekly

Completely change bedding on the cage floor and in the litter box. If the cage has a solid floor, you might need to change bedding more frequently if your rabbit does not consistently use his litter box. Wash and dry the litter box. For hutches, use a shovel or dog pooper scooper to remove droppings. At least once a week, use a narrow flexible brush to clean the slimy film that will develop inside water bottles. Check that sipper tubes are not clogged with bedding or food.

Monthly

Once a month, do a thorough cleaning. Use a vacuum to remove any hairs that are stuck to the cage wires. If necessary, disinfect the cage and the surrounding area. Pet stores sell mild cleansers that are safe for animals. Wash inside the cage with warm, soapy water. Be sure to rinse and dry it thoroughly. Wash water bottles, food dishes, and any plastic toys. Wood toys can eventually splinter if washed in water, scraping grime off of them with a file is effective. Scrape or file off any grime that might have accumulated on the bars of a wire cage. Replace the nest box if needed.

Do not keep your rabbit in the basement or garage. Not only is the garage unhealthy from any automobile exhaust, but both locations are likely to have more extreme and variable temperatures, as well as less suitable lighting. Most importantly, your bunny is likely to be neglected.

Indoor Exercise Pens

In order to stay healthy, your rabbit must be given time to exercise and play outside of his cage. If you do not want to give him roaming privileges in one or more rooms of your house (see Chapter 6 on rabbit proofing), you should buy an indoor exercise pen. Portable pens that fold away for easy storage are sold at pet stores. You can buy one made exclusively for small animals, or if they are unavailable, try the variety sold for dogs or puppies. For the latter types, make sure the space between the bars is not so large your rabbit can escape. To prevent him from hopping out, the pen should be 3 feet (0.9 m) high for small breeds and 4 feet (1.2 m) high for large breeds.

Place the pen on a tarp to protect the floor from any accidents and from any destructive activities such as digging at carpet. An indoor exercise pen provides your rabbit with

a safe environment in which to play. Be sure to supply plenty of toys, as well as a litter box.

Your bunny can play in the pen while you do chores or schoolwork. Do be aware that he will eventually become bored and less active within the same environment, but many pens are large enough for you to comfortably sit in and so you can visit to add some bonding time to these out-of-cage activities.

Grazing Runs

If you have a backyard lawn, a portable grazing run provides an enjoyable means for your rabbit to exercise and graze on fresh grass during nice weather. Most are lightweight and can be moved each day to a new grazing area. Never let your rabbit graze on a lawn

Rabbits love attention and need to be part of family activities or they become lonely and may engage in destructive behaviors.

that has been treated with pesticides or weed killers. Also, a portion of the run must remain in the shade during the time your rabbit is outside. Because of sensitivity to hot weather, only place him outside when temperatures have cooled below 85°F (29.4°C).

For security, most rabbits appreciate a nest box in their run. Rather than taking the nest box out of your rabbit's inside cage, a cardboard box can be used outdoors. To prevent a gut ache from eating too much grass, only allow your rabbit a 10-15 minute outing per day. If he does not develop diarrhea, slowly increase the amount of time he spends in his run. Because being outdoors is new and potentially scary, stay close by and visit with your rabbit until he is relaxed and comfortable in his new surroundings. Although it's never a good idea to leave your pet unsupervised, you must be certain he is safe from any other pets you have and from any neighborhood animals that can gain access to your yard if you must leave him unattended in a run.

There is no commercial manufacturer of grazing runs, so you must construct one yourself. Sometimes called a grazing ark, the run consists of a light-weight wood frame covered with a heavy, wire mesh with spaces no larger than ½ inch x 2 inches (1.27 cm x 5.1 cm). You can make the run with four sides and a top, or with four sides, a top, a bottom, and a large door with a latch. The first type is not as secure because it must be pegged down so a rabbit cannot tip it over, and

Always supervise your rabbit's outdoor time, and be sure he is kept away from toxic plants or chemically treated grass.

without a wire mesh bottom, a rabbit can burrow and potentially escape. It's also not compatible with a perfect lawn as a rabbit may dig a shallow scrape in which to stay cool and rest. A wire mesh floor can prevent these potential problems.

Outdoor Housing

Hutches

If your rabbit is going to be kept outdoors, he needs to be housed in a hutch. Hutches cost considerably more than indoor cages. Commercially made

Rabbit Activity Cycles

Rabbits are crepuscular, which means they are most active in the early morning and in the early evening. Nights and mornings are their main feeding times. At night, your rabbit will hop about, eat his food, drink water, and make other noises. However, he will also sleep. During the day, your rabbit will snooze, waiting for you to come home and take him out to play. If you want to make him truly happy, be sure he is allowed out of his cage around dawn and dusk.

a raccoon to reach inside. A common mesh size is ½ inch x 1 inch (1.27 cm x 2.5 cm). As with an indoor cage, a rabbit housed on a wire floor must be provided with a section of solid floor.

There are pros and cons for choosing a wood versus metal hutch. Those constructed of wood can be difficult to keep clean because they tend to absorb urine and other odors. If washed with water, the wood can swell and split. Plenty of time must be allowed for it to dry before returning your rabbit to his home. The interior should be covered with a wire mesh to prevent gnawing. On the other hand, metal hutches can be lightweight and easy to clean. However, the metal retains heat during hot weather and cold during cold weather.

The minimum size hutch to buy is based on the formula of one square foot per one pound (0.3 sq m per 0.5 kg) of rabbit. Thus, a 5 pound rabbit needs five square feet of space. However, providing the largest size hutch you can afford is always best. It must have room for food dishes, water bottles, and toys. If you have two rabbits, double the minimum cage size.

Weatherproofing

A reliable hutch should be weatherproof, with three solid walls and a wire mesh front. It should have a waterproof, sloping roof that overhangs sufficiently to protect the sides of the enclosure. You must be able to easily reach inside to all areas within. Besides a front door, the hutch should also have a top door to facilitate access. Be

hutches constructed of either wood and wire mesh or metal and wire mesh are commonly sold at pet and feed stores. No matter what materials they are constructed with, from functional metal to fancy wood that resembles a log cabin, high-quality hutches should share certain necessary design features. All types should have wire mesh floors that allow droppings to fall out of the enclosure. However, the mesh must not be large enough for the rabbit's foot to fall through, or large enough for a nimble-handed predator such as

Be sure that outdoor housing is secure and that it provides adequate protection from extremes in weather.

Outdoor enclosures must protect your animal from wind, rain, snow, sun, heat, and high humidity. A well-designed hutch can only perform these functions if it is properly located. It helps to know the pattern of sun, shade, and wind in your yard so you can select a good site. While a hutch can be moved at a later time, it can be a cumbersome process. It should be shaded and protected from direct sunlight, although an hour of morning or late afternoon sun is not harmful in temperate climates.

In many parts of the country, keeping an outside rabbit sufficiently warm in winter and cool in summer is difficult. You can make additional modifications to the environment with heavy canvas tarps in winter and cooling shade

aware that the height of the enclosure can affect your access through the top opening. However, a hutch should not rest directly on the ground. Tall hutches are thought to provide the best protection from potential predators that could harass your rabbit.

A nest box is essential in an outdoor enclosure and provides your rabbit with protection from uncomfortable weather and security when threatened. Most hutches have a nest box built onto one end. However, if the model you buy doesn't have one, you must provide it. In summer, it must be well ventilated to protect your rabbit from heat stress.

Bunny Benefit

If you are a gardener, rabbit keeping can help your garden bloom. Droppings, litter box contents, and dirty bedding can be added to a compost pile. They will break down in the same way as other materials and form moist rich soil. Old bedding can also be used around the base of plants to help keep soil moist.

An outdoor hutch should be kept in a location that will make regular interaction with your rabbit easy; if isolated, he will become lonely and fearful.

cloths in summer. Both items can be purchased at hardware and garden stores.

Rabbits tolerate cold better than heat and can acclimate to colder weather over a period of time. However, in areas with days of freezing temperatures, the hutch might need to be moved inside to a shed or other building, or provided with a heater. A heat source is also necessary so that drinking water remains unfrozen. Since most heat sources require an electrical outlet, the hutch must be sited accordingly. Dwarf and small breeds less than 5 pounds (2.3 kg) are not hardy enough to be housed outdoors during cold weather without heat.

Conversely, temperatures above 85°F (29.4°C), especially in conjunction with high humidity, can lead to heat stress. In such climates, you might need to modify a hutch to increase air flow. For example, a small battery operated fan can direct air across one end of the enclosure. You can also place a frozen bottle of water inside the hutch each day until the weather cools.

Location

An additional consideration is that the hutch should be located where it will be easy for you to regularly interact with your rabbit. Ideally, you should be able to see your pet from your house. Do not place the hutch in an out-of-the way part of the yard where your rabbit will be more isolated and the chances for neglect are increased. At the same time, it should not be sited in a location that is excessively noisy.

Safety

Purchasing a large, well-constructed hutch is of the utmost importance. Do not buy one constructed with chicken wire as it is too flimsy to keep your rabbit secure from potential predators. Many outdoor pet rabbits are killed by other family pets, such as a dog with a high prey drive that shares the backyard with a rabbit during the day and has plenty of time to figure out how to get him.

Your rabbit must also be protected from urban-adapted wildlife such as coyotes and raccoons. If you live in an area with these species, buy a tall enclosure to minimize a predator's ability to scare your rabbit to death by looking into his home. Do not place the hutch next to a fence or under a tree that an agile animal could use to jump onto the roof. Using his sense of hearing and smell, your rabbit can tell when a predator is nearby without even seeing the animal. A frightened rabbit can panic and hurt himself while leaping around. If your yard is part of the home range of potential predators—for example, you regularly see raccoons or coyotes at night—it is unwise to keep rabbits outside.

Cage Cleaning and Supplies

No matter how much a rabbit grooms himself, if the cage is dirty, he cannot keep himself clean. Rabbits have no offensive odors; however, their cage will smell if it is not cleaned often enough. While most droppings do not smell bad, urine can develop a pungent odor from ammonia. Bedding products designed to control or eliminate odor can be used to minimize this. However, no odor-control product can solve the problem of urine and droppings accumulating in the cage due to improper maintenance.

The ammonia vapors that develop from urine can make owning a rabbit less pleasant, but you must realize that it is also uncomfortable for your pet. Ammonia is a severe irritant and is detrimental to his health. It affects the mucous membranes of the eyes and respiratory tract and can lead to a respiratory ailment. It leaves a rabbit open to other opportunistic infections as well. Housed on dirty, moist

Outdoor Rabbits

The best time of year to purchase an outside rabbit is when you have the most time to play with him and the weather encourages outdoor activity. Because rabbits kept outside have less social interaction, strongly consider purchasing two at the same time to keep each other company (see Chapter 1). Remember, a rabbit that is neglected and lonely will become shy and fearful. Also, regardless of how fancy the hutch or cage may be, take every precaution to be sure it is predator-proof and escape-proof.

bedding, even for a day, leaves him susceptible to these problems. If you can smell your pet's home, then it is certainly an unhealthy environment.

By maintaining a consistent cleaning schedule, you can prevent the task from becoming overwhelming. If you visit with your rabbit while you clean his home, the chore will not be as tedious. Always have fresh bedding available so you do not postpone cleaning and expose your rabbit to an unhealthy environment. Remember, this pet has become a member of your family, and he deserves to live in a clean and comfortable home just as you do.

FAMILY-FRIENDLY TIP

Children and Pet Care

Owning a pet is one of the pleasures of childhood. Besides being fun, pets can also help teach children respect for other living creatures. They allow children to assume responsibility and develop nurturing skills, as well as learning how to be compassionate, how to play gently, and what hurting means.

Raising a pet from a young animal to adulthood can be a rewarding experience. Children can be proud of their pets and enjoy the process of discovery that comes from caring for them. However, these benefits are unlikely to occur without a parent's involvement. Age and maturity are important factors when deciding how much responsibility a child can assume. Parents of younger children must be aware that the rabbit's welfare will be their responsibility as well. They often tell their children, "OK, you can get it, but don't expect me to help you care for it," but, depending on the child's age, this is an unrealistic expectation. While it is understandable that busy parents do not welcome additional responsibilities, a rabbit cannot teach a child to be responsible. To a varying extent, a parent must participate in the pet's care. Such assistance might include driving to the pet store to buy fresh food, supervising playtime to ensure the safety of the child and rabbit, or helping to clean a large cage that a small child has trouble managing.

Because children cannot be expected to care for their pets without supervision, it helps if a parent is enthusiastic about the pet. Unsupportive parents can make it more difficult. Simply by showing an interest, they can encourage their child to properly care for his rabbit.

Chapter 3

Good Eating

Over the last ten years, more and more people have come to regard their pets as important family members. This rise in esteem was not reserved for just dogs and cats, but also extended to other pets such as rabbits. Spurred in part by information acquired from veterinarians who treated rabbits that were overweight or had gastrointestinal diseases, as well as breeders and rescue groups, a better understanding of their dietary needs emerged.

A diet of alfalfa pellets was originally designed to safely and conveniently put weight on rabbits raised for the meat and fur trade. Longevity was not a concern for commercial "rabbit ranchers," whereas a long healthy life is something pet owners desire for their animals. Because of potential health problems tied to diet, many authorities concluded that alfalfa pellets were not the best food for pet rabbits. However, manufacturers responded by developing different pellet formulas made specifically for them. Consequently, there are now a variety of packaged foods with different amounts of nutrients available.

Although there are more choices, there still is no unanimous agreement among veterinarians, breeders, hobbyists, and rescue groups as to the best diet for pet rabbits. Nonetheless, with some caveats, you can typically purchase a bag of nutritionally dense rabbit pellets, feed them according to the directions, and your rabbit should be fine. It is also important to include hay and fresh vegetables to provide a fully balanced diet, which is discussed later in more detail.

Basic Nutrition

Good nutrition is a key factor in promoting a long and healthy life for your rabbit. A balanced diet includes the appropriate amounts of protein, carbohydrates, fat, vitamins, and minerals. All these nutrients interact in the growth, maintenance, and functioning of an animal's body.

Protein is needed for functions such as the growth and maintenance of muscle, and the production

The Expert Knows

Unhealthy Foods

Some of the pet rabbit's biggest potential health problems have to do with digestive disorders caused by improper diet. While it can be fun to offer new types of food and see if your pet enjoys them, many are highly unsuitable. Herbivorous rabbits won't eat just apples and carrots, but will happily munch pizza crusts, crackers, and other human foods. They also have a strong sweet tooth and will gladly eat chocolate, cookies, and other items that are downright bad for them. All these foods are very unhealthy, and your rabbit should not be allowed to eat them. Other unhealthy foods include the kibble in a dog's or cat's dish, both of which are too high in protein for your rabbit.

of antibodies, hormones, and enzymes. The amount of protein that your pet needs is influenced by a number of physiological factors, such as age and reproductive status. Rabbits older than six months need less protein than when they are in their most active growth period.

Good Eating

Pregnant or nursing rabbits require increased protein.

Carbohydrates perform numerous functions, such as providing energy. Concentrated sources of carbohydrates include grains like oats and corn. Fat is a concentrated source of energy that provides twice as many calories per serving as protein or carbohydrates. It makes up part of the structure of every cell and is necessary for absorption of fat-soluble vitamins, such as vitamins A and D. As a source of essential fatty acids, it helps provide your rabbit with a healthy coat and skin. A deficiency of fat can show up as scaly skin, or rough, thin hair.

Vitamins are necessary as catalysts for chemical reactions in the body. They are important in preventing diseases and in regulating functions such as growth and blood clotting.

They are classified as water-soluble or as fat-soluble.

Minerals, which include calcium, phosphorous, sodium, and other chemical elements, are important in many body functions, such as the development of bones and teeth, muscle and nerve function, and proper water balance. A deficiency or excess can lead to serious medical problems. Trace elements, which include cobalt, copper, iodine, iron, manganese, selenium, and zinc, are necessary nutrients, but only in very small amounts. Trace elements perform many functions, such as the role of iron bringing oxygen to the body.

Fiber and Digestion

Fiber is an important part of a rabbit's daily diet and is essential for normal digestion. Also called roughage, it is the indigestible part of plants.

Nutritional needs are determined by stages of life; for example, babies and nursing moms need additional protein.

Fiber is needed to stimulate the gastrointestinal tract and to promote the movement of food so digestion can occur. Without sufficient fiber, the movement of food through the digestive tract can slow or stop. This can lead to potentially life-threatening intestinal disease.

Rabbits are hindgut fermenters. They digest much of their food in the cecum, which is a sac about ten times larger than the rabbit's stomach. The cecum is located at the juncture of the small intestine and large intestine, which is the same location as a person's appendix. At this juncture, most of the semi-digested food passes into the cecum, while the indigestible fiber moves into the large intestine, also called the colon. Water is absorbed from the material in the colon, and then the remaining matter is expelled about four to five hours later as round, hard droppings.

Meanwhile, in the cecum, bacteria and protozoa ferment digestible fiber and other parts of the food into proteins, essential fatty acids, B-complex vitamins, and vitamin K. The contents of the cecum are then excreted about eight to nine hours

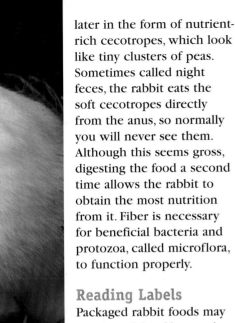

later in the form of nutrient-rich cecotropes, which look like tiny clusters of peas. Sometimes called night feces, the rabbit eats the soft cecotropes directly from the anus, so normally you will never see them. Although this seems gross, digesting the food a second time allows the rabbit to obtain the most nutrition from it. Fiber is necessary for beneficial bacteria and protozoa, called microflora, to function properly.

Reading Labels

Packaged rabbit foods may consist solely of hay, such as alfalfa or timothy, or they can be a pellet mix made with hay, grains, and added vitamins and minerals.

Pellets are formulated to be nutritionally complete. The items that compose a food are stated in the ingredients list in descending order by weight. The first three to five items listed make up most of the food.

On every bag of rabbit food is a guaranteed analysis that gives the percentage of nutrients contained in it, such as protein, fat, and calcium, as well as fiber and moisture. The protein and fat contents are usually listed as minimums, while the amount of fiber and calcium are typically given as both minimums and maximums. The word "crude," which precedes each measure, refers to laboratory analysis rather

than digestibility. Even commercial treats sold at pet stores provide basic nutritional information on protein, fat, fiber, and moisture content.

Reading the nutritional analysis for pelleted foods can seem unnecessarily complex compared to simply purchasing a bag of pellets from a convenient source and feeding them to your pet. However, providing the appropriate food can help to prevent and manage some health problems that afflict pet rabbits. For example, the incidence of obesity, diarrhea, and hairballs can be reduced

Feeding Schedule

Rabbits are creatures of routine and do best with regularly scheduled mealtimes. Plan on feeding your bunny twice a day—once in the morning and once in the evening. Many owners find it convenient to feed their pets before they leave for school or work and shortly before or after their own evening meals. Of course, schedules are occasionally broken. If you know you will return home later than usual in the evening, provide your rabbit with extra hay in the morning.

in pet rabbits that are fed a high-fiber (at least 17 percent) and low-protein diet (12-14 percent).

Types of Food

Your rabbit should be fed a combination of dry and moist foods. Dry foods include pellets, hay, and grains such as barley and oats. Pet and feed stores sell various types of dry packaged food for rabbits. Moist foods include fresh vegetables, fruits, and any plants your pet eats when you allow him outside in a grazing run. You can buy moist food while shopping in grocery stores.

Dry Food

Pellets

Commercial pellets should be a staple food for your pet rabbit. They are convenient to feed, nutritionally balanced, and their hardness helps keep teeth trimmed. Currently, pellets are based on either alfalfa or timothy hay. Those made mostly with alfalfa are typically higher in protein than pellets made with timothy hay. Other ingredients, such as grains, can increase the protein level.

Some pellet mixes are sold as gourmet blends that include

other ingredients such as whole grains, kibble, and dried fruits and vegetables. The ingredients are balanced so a rabbit cannot eat an excess of any item, such as oats or dried bananas. However, if he picks out the tasty tidbits, leaves the hay pellets, and waits for you to refill his bowl, he is likely to end up with a poorly balanced diet and serious health problems. For this reason, some veterinarians and breeders recommend against feeding gourmet mixes. If you choose to feed a fancy food, you must exercise prudence and restraint.

Adult pet rabbits can be fed a pellet that ranges from 13 to 16 percent crude protein. Growing rabbits and pregnant and lactating does can be fed higher protein pellets, up to 18 percent. However, once a young rabbit is grown, between five and twelve months and depending

Strictly Vegetarian

Remember that rabbits are vegetarians in the wild. For optimum health, they will need a balanced and varied diet in order to obtain the necessary nutrients to stay healthy. You will need to provide fresh vegetables and fruits, and most importantly, roughage, in addition to a pelleted diet.

Senior Diets

A middle-aged or senior bunny (more than six years of age) should continue the adult diet if he maintains a healthy, stable weight. The amount of pellets fed can be varied as needed. Geriatric rabbits may need unrestricted pellets to keep their weight up. Alfalfa can be given to those that are underweight, but only if calcium levels are monitored. An annual veterinary checkup can determine any special needs or nutritional deficiencies.

on the breed, he should be switched to a lower protein pellet. Likewise, a doe should also be switched to lower protein pellets after her young are weaned. When changing to a different type of pellet, gradually mix the new food in with the old. A complete change in feed can usually be made over one week.

Avoid buying pellet foods higher than 18 percent protein. Such pellets, sometimes labeled performance foods, are more appropriate for achieving maximum growth and weight gain in rabbits that are raised for meat and fur. Whatever brand you select, a good general rule is that the fiber level should always be higher than the protein level. Depending on the

Got Water?!

Rabbits drink a lot of water, between 1 ½ to 4 ½ ounces (44.4-133.1 ml) of water per 2 ½ pounds (1.13 kg) of body weight each day. A rabbit that weighs 4 ½ pounds (2.04 kg) drinks as much water as a dog that weighs 22 pounds (9.97 kg)! You don't want your pet to run out of water. A rabbit can survive several days without food, but a day without water can cause dehydration and even lead to death. Many water bottles are sold with milliliter or ounce markings on them. (There are approximately 29.5 milliliters in one ounce.) Such markings are useful to track water consumption.

The amount of water a rabbit drinks each day depends on the type of food he eats. For example, a rabbit fed a diet high in fiber or protein needs more water than one fed a low fiber or protein diet. A rabbit primarily fed a diet of fresh vegetables, which naturally have high water content, will drink less water than one fed a diet of pellets.

Water is also necessary to deliver nutrients to the cells in the body and is essential to the proper functioning of the body's organs and systems. Be sure your rabbit is given plenty of fresh water daily.

ingredients and how finely the hay is ground, different brands of pellets have different amounts of fiber. Your rabbit's pellet food should have a fiber level of at least 15 percent or be between 15-17 percent. Pellets with a higher fiber content (18-22 percent) can help prevent obesity.

Do not choose a pellet diet that has a fat content higher than 5 percent. Ideally, fat levels should be 3 percent or less. Nuts, grains, and seeds can contribute to the fat content. A high fat content can contribute to unhealthy weight gain.

All these percentages can seem overwhelming. However, there are specific times you should pay attention to these percentages: when feeding a growing rabbit, when switching a rabbit to an adult diet, and when your veterinarian suggests a specific diet.

Hay

The fiber found in pellets is often not sufficient, so you must supplement them with loose hay. Hay provides essential fiber, which helps prevent potentially life-threatening gastrointestinal problems. It also provides your rabbit with something to do. Some rabbits kept for long periods in their cage become so bored they develop the bad habit of chewing their own fur.

Most large pet stores sell a variety of types in convenient packages. If

Your rabbit should be fed a combination of moist and dry foods, including large amounts of hay.

loose hay is unavailable, cubed hay is better than none at all. Feed stores also sell it, but you will need to buy it by the bale. While it is cheaper, you need a dry place to store it. A bale of hay is quite large, usually 4 feet (1.2 m) long by almost 2 feet (0.6 m) high and 2 feet (0.6 m) wide. The bale must be placed on a wooden pallet to allow air circulation and to prevent mold from growing on the bottom portion. Do not feed hay that got wet or moldy.

There are two types of hay. Grass hay includes orchard grass, oat hay, timothy, and mixed grass. Legume hay includes alfalfa and clover. Young, growing rabbits, pregnant and nursing does, and outdoor rabbits can be fed alfalfa hay. But adult house rabbits kept inside do not need the higher amount of protein, calories, and calcium found in alfalfa and should be fed a grass hay. Rabbits much prefer the tastier leaves and stems of alfalfa hay compared to

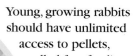

Pellets provide basic nutrition, but need to be supplemented with other healthy foods.

grass hay. Slightly reducing the amount of pellets can encourage a rabbit to eat grass hay, as can offering different types of grass hay.

Young, growing rabbits should have unlimited access to pellets, called free-feeding. Once they are adults, generally between six to eight months, the general rule is to feed ¼ cup (4 oz/113 g) of pellets per 5 pounds (2.3 kg) of body weight divided into two meals per day.

Reducing your rabbit's ration of pellets is important; feeding too many is a major cause of obesity, soft stools, and gastrointestinal health problems.

How Much to Feed

How much your rabbit needs to eat will change throughout his lifetime. The amount will vary depending not only on his age and reproductive status, but also on his activity level. A rabbit that is allowed to run and play outside his cage will require more food than one that sits neglected in his cage day after day.

Most packaged foods come with feeding instructions, and you can use these as a starting point. They are general recommendations, usually based on a rabbit's adult weight. Your animal might need to eat slightly more or less. The proper portion to feed is whatever amount is necessary to maintain optimum weight and condition.

No matter what your rabbit's age, he should always have hay in his cage. Each morning, remove any that remains uneaten before replacing it with fresh hay. Likewise, remove any uneaten pellets. Do not just put new food on top of the old food.

Supplements

A diet containing pellets, unlimited amounts of hay, and a variety of fresh vegetables provides all the vitamins and minerals your rabbit needs. He will also obtain vitamins from ingestion of cecal pellets. Unless your veterinarian recommends a vitamin and mineral supplement for a specific condition, most pet rabbits do not require supplements.

Fresh is Best

It's important that the food you feed your rabbit is fresh. Food that is old can

lose its nutritional value. Pellets that are soft and crumbly are old and stale and should not be fed. Packaged foods should be sweet smelling, not rancid or dusty. Buy no more than one month's supply at a time. Even though it can be cheaper, do not buy large quantities of pelleted food because it will take too long to use up.

Check to see whether there is an expiration date on the package. Some manufacturers stamp a date on the bags and recommend that the food be used within one year of this date. Typically, the freshest, best quality packaged food is found at busy pet and feed stores that constantly turn over their stock.

Store the pellets in a cool, dry environment. Exposure to sunlight, heat, and time degrades the vitamins in food. Keep it in an airtight container, such as a glass jar with a lid, or be sure to completely close a container that is self-sealing. This will keep the food fresh and prevent it from spoiling.

Moist Foods

Vegetables
Rabbits love vegetables, and fresh

The amount you feed will vary depending on age, reproductive status, and activity level.

Vegetables to Avoid

There are some vegetables you should not feed your pet because they can cause gastrointestinal upset. Even if your rabbit seems to eat these vegetables without noticeable problems, it is still best not to include them as they can cause intestinal stasis. Vegetables too high in sugar and starch include any kind of bean, green beans, corn, peas, and potatoes. Other types that should not be fed include cucumber, eggplant, red beets, rhubarb, tomatoes, and zucchini.

foods provide important variety and nutrients in their diet. Eating is their favorite pastime, and munching on veggies is good for them—it can relieve boredom while providing something healthy to do. However, wait to provide a growing bunny with fresh vegetables until he is full grown. Choose dark leafy vegetables, root vegetables, and dark yellow vegetables. Rabbits will relish

Good Eating

for each 4 pounds (1.8 kg) of your rabbit's weight. For example, a 2 pound (0.9 kg) rabbit would be fed ½ cup (8 oz/226.8 g) of vegetables.

Whether you are re-introducing vegetables after a hiatus or feeding a new type of vegetable, remember to slowly start with a small amount, no more than a tablespoon to be safe. Feeding a large amount can cause acute diarrhea. Make sure your rabbit does not develop diarrhea before increasing the amount, which should be done gradually over a period of a week. In addition, feed only one type of vegetable at a time and wait several days before adding other kinds. This way you will know if a particular vegetable causes problems. If it causes soft stools or diarrhea, do not feed it to your rabbit. Certain vegetables, such as cabbage, spinach, cauliflower, and broccoli, can cause digestive upset in some rabbits, while others will be perfectly fine.

You might find your consistency in feeding fresh vegetables changes from week to week. One week you diligently provide them, but the next week you are too busy and forget. Keeping a container of pre-washed, cut veggies in the refrigerator can

It's important to feed your rabbit food that is fresh and to remove uneaten food before it spoils.

salad greens such as endive, escarole, radicchio, spinach, and romaine lettuce. But skip the iceberg lettuce as it is mostly water and provides little nutrition or fiber. They also enjoy fresh herbs such as basil, cilantro, mint, parsley, and peppermint. Herbs can be expensive to buy in a grocery store. If you have space, it is cheaper to grow your own in an herb garden to share with your rabbit.

Ideally, you should provide fresh vegetables each day, but several times a week is better than not at all. You can feed up to 1 cup (16 oz/453.6 g)

make it easier when life gets hectic. Also, bags of pre-cut vegetables are sold at most grocery stores.

Finicky Eaters

Just as people have their own tastes, so do rabbits. If your pet refuses to eat a particular vegetable, don't give up. Try offering it again over several days or wait a few weeks and try again. Most rabbits will quickly consume them. It is very important to remove any uneaten moist foods after a few hours. Any left in the cage can become putrid. Bacteria and mold can grow on them, which could make your pet sick.

In some parts of the country, such as the west coast, a wide variety of vegetables are available year round, while in other locations less variety is present. Use whatever is fresh and easily available, even if you are limited to only a few types. Grocery stores remove produce that is no longer fresh enough to sell, but it can still be perfectly suitable for your rabbit. Some stores will give you as much as you want, if it is for your pet. Just be sure to remove any bad portions before feeding.

Fruits

Even more than vegetables, rabbits love fresh fruits. However, to maintain your pet's svelte figure, sugary fruits should not be overfed. Rabbits can safely eat just about any kind, including kiwis, peaches, and watermelon. High-fiber fruits are best. These include apple, peach,

Healthy Vegetable Choices

alfalfa, radish, and clover sprouts
beet greens
bell peppers
bok choy
broccoli, including leaves and stems
brussel sprouts
carrots and carrot tops
celery, including the leaves
chard
collard
fennel
kale
radish greens
watercress

plum, pear, melon, raspberry, papaya, blueberry, blackberry, strawberry, and pineapple.

Fruits can be expensive, especially when they are not in season. Relatively inexpensive ones such as bananas, grapes, and oranges are other options. All fresh fruit should be washed before feeding. Remove the seeds and stems and any large seed pits. Small amounts of dried fruits such as banana chips and raisins can also be offered.

For rabbits that weigh less than 5 pounds (2.3 kg), feed no more

Feed fresh vegetables and fruits in small quantities to prevent intestinal distress, and be sure to avoid those high in acidity, like tomatoes.

than 1 tablespoon a day. Larger rabbits can be fed up to two tablespoons a day. One tablespoon is not very much. It is worth taking out the measuring spoons every so often to remind yourself of the appropriate portion size. Too much can lead to digestive upset and gastrointestinal stasis, and it can contribute to excess weight.

Preparing a container of pre-washed and sliced fruit can make serving your rabbit easier than if you have to cut it up for him every day. Your pet's fruit salad can consist of several fruits. As with vegetables, always offer new types in very small portions to make sure your rabbit does not experience digestive upset. Rather than feeding them as part of his regular meal, you can use tasty fruits to bond during playtime and training.

Treats

Your rabbit will greet any treats that you give him with delight. And tasty treats are a great way to win his confidence. The best kind is a favorite piece of vegetable or fruit. Another option is sprouted wheat grass, which is available at pet stores. You can also sprout wild bird seed for your rabbit to snack on once the plants are several inches high. Green plants from your backyard, such as a handful of fresh grass or some dandelion leaves and their flowers will be relished by your bunny. But be sure they are safe and not poisonous before offering them.

If you collect plants from your neighborhood or countryside, be sure that no pesticides or herbicides were sprayed on them. Do not collect from roadsides with a lot of traffic due to pollution, or from locations where wild rabbits live as disease transmission could be a problem.

Many owners enjoy buying the various commercial rabbit treats sold in pet stores, such as honey-coated seed and nut sticks, dehydrated fruit and vegetable puffs, and nut cakes. Some come in attractive shapes and colors designed to appeal to people, not rabbits. Their packages often claim the product is healthful and nutritious. However, many of these treats are too high in fat and sugar. They should only be offered on special occasions and in moderation.

If you feed a "gourmet mix" pellet food, it is best to not feed treats other than fresh vegetables because these mixes already contain treat foods. If you prefer to also feed commercial treats, then switch the main diet to a plain pellet.

Why should you be concerned about feeding too many treats, the wrong kind of treat, or allowing your rabbit to eat treat foods that are high in protein and carbohydrates and low in fiber? Because a simple gut ache is not the likely result; rather junk food treats can cause gastrointestinal

FAMILY-FRIENDLY TIP

Set Feeding Guidelines

Parents should not give their child feeding tasks that are too difficult. Preschoolers can help with simple tasks such as pouring pre-measured food into the rabbit's dish. Elementary age children (six to nine years) can assume more responsibility. For example, they can feed and water the rabbit and remind their parents when fresh supplies are needed. Children ten and older can usually assume almost full responsibility, although parents should still oversee care to make sure the pet is not neglected.

diseases that can be deadly for your pet rabbit.

The Overweight Rabbit

If your rabbit is a purebred, the breed standard will let you know the weight he should be when fully grown (see Table 1 in Chapter 1). If he is a mixed breed, your veterinarian can help you determine his ideal weight. Keeping a monthly record of your rabbit's weight will help you monitor his well-being. Some scales are sensitive enough to give the weight of small rabbits. If

Avoid feeding too many sugary fruits as they can contribute to excess weight; high-fiber fruits like apples are best.

yours is not, you can weigh yourself and then weigh yourself again while holding your pet. Subtracting the difference between the two weights will provide his weight.

In between monthly weigh-ins, you can still tell if your rabbit is receiving the right amount of food. You should not be able to easily feel his backbone and hip bones, nor should they be covered by a thick layer of fat so that they are difficult to feel. If your rabbit is thin, give him

more to eat. If he is overweight, give him more hay, and eliminate treats. A healthy weight is crucial to your pet's longevity.

It can be difficult to control how much food a rabbit eats if there is more than one animal in a cage. The dominant individual can sometimes eat food meant for the subordinate cagemates. In such a case, you might need to separate the rabbits into two cages, but you can place them side by side so they can still visit.

Many plants are poisonous to rabbits. It is safest to completely remove them from the areas in which your rabbit lives and plays. A list of many, but not all, of these follows:

almond
aloe
amaryllis (bulbs)
anemone
angel's trumpet
apple (seeds)
apricot (all parts except fruit)
asparagus fern
autumn crocus
avocado
balsam pear (seeds, outer rind of fruit)
baneberry (berries, roots)
begonia
betel-nut palm
bird of paradise (seeds)
bitter cherry (seeds)
bittersweet
black nightshade
black walnut (hulls)
bloodroot
bluebonnet
buttercup (leaves)
black locust
boxwood (leaves, twigs)
bracken fern
buckeye (seeds)
buckthorn
bull nettle
caladium
calendula
calico bush
carnation
carolina jessamine
celastrus
ceriman
cherry tree (bark, twig, leaves, pits)
chinaberry tree
chinese bellflower
chinese lantern
chinese evergreen
choke cherry (seeds)
christmas candle (sap)
christmas rose
chrysanthemum
clematis
climbing nightshade
coffee bean
cone flower
coral plant (seeds)
cordatum
corn plant
cowbane
cuban laurel

cuckoopint
cyclamen
daffodil (bulbs)
daisy
daphne (berries, bark)
datura (berries)
deadly amanita
deadly nightshade
death camas
delphinium
dieffenbachia (leaves)
dogbane
dutchman's breeches
eggplant (all but fruit)
elderberry (unripe berries, roots, stems)
elephant ear (leaves, stem)
english laurel
false hellebore
false henbane
false parsley
fireweed
florida beauty
flowering maple
foxglove (leaves, seeds)
garden sorrel
geranium
ghostweed
giant touch-me-not
gladiola
golden chain
golden pothos
green gold
hawaiian ti
hemlock
henbane (seeds)
hogwart
holly (berries)
horse chestnut (nuts, twigs)
horsetail reed
hurricane plant
hyacinth (bulbs)
hydrangea
impatiens
indian hemp
indian rubber
indian turnip
indigo
inkberry
iris (bulbs)
ivy
jack-in-the-pulpit
japanese euonymus
japanese yew

jasmine
java bean (uncooked)
jerusalem cherry (berries)
jessamine
jimson weed (leaves, seeds)
johnson grass
jonquil
juniper (needles, stems, berries)
laburnum
lace fern
lacy tree philodendron
lady slipper
larkspur
laurel
laurel cherry
lily (all types)
lobelia
locoweed
lords and ladies
lupine
macadamia nut
marbel queen
marsh marigold
mayapple
meadow saffron
medicine plant
mesquite
mexican breadfruit
mescal bean (seeds)
milk bush
milkweed
mistletoe (berries)
mock orange (fruit)
monkshood (leaves, roots)
moonflower
morning glory
mother-in-law
mountain laurel
nandina
narcissus (bulbs)
nephytis
nicotania
nightshades (berries, leaves)
nutmeg
oak (acorns, foliage)
oleander (leaves, branches, nectar)
oxalis
panda
patience plant
peach (leaves, twigs, seeds)

pear (seeds)
peony
periwinkle
peyote
philodendron
plum (seeds)
plumosa fern
poinsettia (leaves, flowers)
poison ivy
poison oak
poison sumac
pokeweed
poppy
potato (eyes & new shoots, green parts)
precatory bean
primrose
primula
privet
queensland nut
ranunculus
red princess
rhododendron
rhubarb (leaves
ribbon plant
rosary pea (seeds)
sago palm schefflera
sennabean
shamrock plant
skunk cabbage
snake palm
snowdrop
solomon's seal
spindleberry
star of bethlehem
stinkweed
sweet pea (seeds & fruit)
tansy
thornapple
toadstools
tomato (leaves, vines)
tree philodendron
tulip (bulb)
umbrella plant
vinca
virginia creeper (berries, sap)
walnuts (hulls, green shells)
wisteria
wood-rose
yellow jasmine
yew (needles, seeds, berries)
yucca

(The parts of the plants to avoid are included in parentheses.)

Chapter 4

Looking Good

Rabbits are naturally clean. They spend up to 20 percent of their waking hours grooming themselves, washing their faces, delicately cleaning each ear with their hind foot, then using their tongue to clean their paws, and even scrubbing the rest of their bodies—front and back. A rabbit that does not groom himself or cannot keep himself clean is probably sick and should be examined by a veterinarian.

Naturally clean, rabbits spend much of their time grooming themselves.

Brushing

All furry animals shed hair, your rabbit included. House rabbits shed throughout the year, but some shed more in fall and spring. Usually, at least once a year, a rabbit will molt heavily for several weeks. In particular, outdoor rabbits will molt their heavy winter coats each spring. During his molt, your rabbit's fur will look patchy. Brushing him will help keep him from swallowing excess hair, especially at this time. It will also reduce the amount of fur drifting about your house and clinging to his cage. Moreover, brushing can be a quiet bonding time with your pet.

A short-haired rabbit should be groomed at least once a week. You can brush him while he sits on your lap or while he is on the floor. Be careful about placing him on a table or other high surface as he may decide to jump off unexpectedly and could become injured. Gently brush the fur in the direction it grows. Do not brush hard

Cutting the Quick

Even professionals will occasionally cut into the quick when trimming nails. If this happens, don't panic. If you don't have styptic powder on hand, you can apply a pinch of flour or cornstarch to the nail to stop the bleeding.

Grooming as a Health Check

Grooming sessions aren't just for appearance's sake, they are a good time to monitor your rabbit's health and well-being. Be sure to notice whether he has a rough coat, dry skin, lumps (especially along his jaw), scabs, or evidence of external parasites, such as flea dirt. Also, make it a habit to check his eyes and inside his ears. If you notice anything unusual, your pet may need to see a vet.

as your rabbit has sensitive skin. He may become fearful of being brushed if it is painful. Use soft brushes such as a rubber brush, a soft-bristle brush, or a grooming glove when he is not shedding much. When your rabbit is molting, use a wire slicker brush.

Long-haired rabbits, including angoras, the Jersey Wooly, or any mixed breed with long hair, need daily grooming with a wire slicker brush and wide tooth comb. This takes dedication and time. Their long hairs are so fine that they will quickly form knots if you skip regular grooming. Long-haired rabbits typically shed heavily once every three months; in between, they will shed more lightly.

During heavy molts, your rabbit should be sheared with clippers, or you can hand-pluck the old fur. To pluck, take hold of some fur using your

forefinger and thumb, and give a gentle tug. You can usually see the new coat coming in underneath the removed fur. If done correctly, plucking should not be painful. But rabbits don't always like it, so don't plan on doing your whole rabbit in one day. You should also reward him with some pleasurable strokes on his head or cheeks during this process.

Bathing

You might wonder if you should bathe your rabbit. If he is dirty and smelly, it is usually because he has been lying on dirty bedding. Cleaning his cage, providing fresh, sweet-smelling bedding, and allowing your rabbit to groom himself is usually better than a bath. However, if he has been sick or had loose droppings, you

71

Grooming Tools

Before grooming your rabbit, be sure that you have the right tools on hand:

rubber brush
soft-bristle brush
wire slicker brush
grooming glove
flea comb
wide tooth comb
    (for long-haired rabbits)
nail trimmers
styptic powder
cotton swabs

Regularly brushing your rabbit's fur helps to keep it healthy and shiny.

might need to clean the area around his hind end. This can be done by spot cleaning him using a warm cloth, followed by a dry cloth to absorb the moisture.

Nail Care

Just like your own nails, the nails of your rabbit grow continuously. Many owners find that long, sharp nails can make handling their pets unpleasant at times. Besides being sharp on human skin, they present a hazard to a rabbit that is allowed to roam loose in the house. They can get caught in carpeting, and your pet's unnoticed struggles can cause the nail to rip or tear out by the root.

Clipping the nails on a regular basis will not only help reduce the likelihood of getting scratched, it will also protect your rabbit from mishaps. You can use clippers designed for birds or cats. Make sure the clippers are sharp as it will make the task much easier. Keep cotton swabs and some type of styptic powder

nearby to stop any bleeding. The best time to trim your rabbit's nails is when he is tired, not when he is wide awake and playful. Using two people is usually best—one to hold the rabbit and one to clip the nails. Always be sure to keep the wound powder and some damp cotton swabs nearby. Although your rabbit will eventually learn to tolerate nail-clipping, try to make each

FAMILY-FRIENDLY TIP

Bonding Time

Children can help groom a rabbit by gently brushing him under adult supervision. After a child has demonstrated that he or she can handle the animal carefully without harming him, he can be allowed to groom the pet regularly. Grooming also provides a quiet time for some gentle bonding during which the bunny can grow to trust the child.

Fleas

Fleas don't just make your rabbit uncomfortable, they can quickly cause him to become anemic, a life-threatening condition. Strive to prevent this problem before it begins by grooming regularly and maintaining clean conditions in your pet's enclosure. A flea comb can be used to remove fleas without resorting to the use of chemicals. Although not usually common on rabbits, fleas can be transmitted by other pets, so it's a good idea to check for them periodically just to be sure.

session as pleasent for him as possible, and be sure to reward him with extra petting.

Because trimming a rabbit's nails can sometimes be difficult, and if done improperly, painful and traumatic, it is often best to have a veterinarian show you how to do it.

Ear Care

Rabbits can get ear mites. If left untreated, mite infestations can cause serious problems. Take your rabbit to a veterinarian if you notice excessive scratching, heavy wax buildup, discharge, redness, swelling, or odor. The most effective treatment and advice on remedying the problem is available from a veterinarian. Do not automatically assume any discharge is from ear mites and try to treat him with a medication sold at pet stores. Accurate diagnosis of the condition will speed your rabbit's recovery and save him from discomfort and pain.

You should examine your rabbit's ears every few weeks. You can gently clean the outer ears with a cotton swab and a veterinary ear cleanser. The wax in the external ear should be carefully removed, without going into the ear canal.

Besides being the cutest part of any bunny, the ears are one of the most important parts of the animal on which to maintain good grooming practices.

As part of your grooming routine, examine your pet's ears, eyes, and teeth weekly.

Chapter 5

Feeling Good

When purchased from a reliable source and given good care, the typical rabbit is hardy and resilient. However, even with all the best precautionary measures, he may still become ill. The reasons a rabbit becomes sick are often due to a combination of factors. For example, a poorly ventilated cage can create a noxious-smelling environment, with high levels of ammonia that can cause an outbreak of a latent respiratory ailment. Numerous variables can affect how sick the rabbit will get, such as his age, dietary deficiencies, or if he is already sick with another illness.

Your pet rabbit is dependent on you for his good health and well-being.

Finding a Veterinarian

In order for your rabbit to receive the proper treatment, he needs to be correctly diagnosed. A veterinarian who routinely treats rabbits and has a special interest in their care is best qualified and will most likely have the necessary, smaller-sized equipment. Such individuals are more likely to be aware of advances and changes in treatment protocol.

Veterinarians who specialize in rabbits can be easier to find in some areas of the country than in others (such as in urban areas compared to rural areas). To locate a qualified veterinarian, you can check with the American Veterinary Medical Association at www.avma.org. You can also inquire at local veterinarians' offices, breeders, critter clubs, rescue groups such as the House Rabbit Society (www.rabbit.org), and pet stores.

Cost Concerns

Even when you recognize that your rabbit is under the weather, you might hesitate to take him to a veterinarian due to the potential expense. Such a visit can be costly, and many owners, or the parents of a child who has a rabbit, find it difficult to spend large sums of money on a pet that is relatively inexpensive. Therefore, it is important that you consider the cost of caring for him throughout the course of his lifetime before deciding to bring him home. If you cannot take on this commitment to your pet's well-being and good health, which is part of being a responsible owner, it's best not to get one in the first place.

At some point, it may become necessary to provide medical intervention and treatment to help a sick or injured pet. If you are concerned about costs, you can discuss them with your veterinarian beforehand. He may offer options such as payment plans or may be able to guide you to some pet insurance programs that are now available.

Be cautious about seeking aid from pet store employees or rescue groups before taking your rabbit to a veterinarian. Although they might be helpful and able to give an educated guess, the expertise, diagnostic skills, and medication needed to treat your rabbit are only available from a professional. Keep in mind that the sicker a rabbit is, the more likely he is to be traumatized from the procedures at a veterinarian's office. Prompt medical attention is the best guarantee of a successful outcome.

The Vet Visit

Rabbits do not need any vaccinations that require an annual visit to the veterinarian. Nonetheless, taking your

pet for an annual physical exam is prudent—even if he is not sick. By listening to his heart, checking for swellings, examining the teeth, and so forth, your vet can detect a disease in its early stages when it is more likely to be cured.

Be prepared to describe your rabbit's housing and feeding regimes. Sometimes, your vet might request that you bring your rabbit in with his

Prevention

It is a truism, but prevention is far better than treatment. When properly cared for, rabbits are less stressed and have better natural resistance to diseases. Prevention is based on common-sense husbandry practices. A plethora of problems can affect rabbits due to poor husbandry—a big word for how a pet is taken care of, including aspects such as housing, food, and water. Your rabbit cannot modify the size, temperature, air circulation, and cleanliness of his home. He is completely dependent upon you to provide him with a proper environment that will ensure his well-being and good health.

Be Prepared

Finding a good vet is one of the most important things you will ever do for your rabbit. No matter how good his home care is on a day-to-day basis, all can be lost if he is entrusted to a vet without the necessary expertise for your type of animal, especially in an emergency. It may even cost the life of your pet. Don't wait for a crisis. When you bring home your rabbit, locate vets in your area and make some calls. Don't be afraid to ask questions, and do your research to be sure he will get the best possible care.

cage, or have a photograph of the cage setup so that his environment can be assessed. Otherwise, you should use a carrier, which is available at pet stores. He or she can also keep you up to date on any important changes in the current understanding of how pet rabbits should be cared for.

Once your rabbit is a senior at about 5 to 6 years of age, it is usually recommended that he get checkups once every 6 months. By analyzing urine and blood samples, your vet can establish a baseline function for your pet's health. The results can be compared with information obtained during future visits. Any changes could indicate illness, which can then be dealt with in a timely fashion.

General Signs of Illness

It is important to always take note of any changes in your rabbit's appearance or behavior, because they can sometimes be indicators of a health problem. Obvious signs of illness include runny nose, watery eyes, and labored breathing. Diarrhea and constipation are also symptoms.

Rabbits are fastidious and like to keep themselves clean; therefore, a dirty matted coat means something is wrong. Sudden changes in behavior such as huddling in a corner, lethargy, reduced appetite, or not eating may indicate a serious problem exists or could be looming. Signs of disease that are more difficult to detect include rough hair, hunched posture, constipation, and weight loss. Particular attention should be paid if a rabbit is sensitive when touched on certain part of his body.

Warning Signs

Pay attention to your rabbit's physical condition and behavior. Note any weight changes, check teeth alignment, and feel for lumps and bumps. Significant changes in the amount of food or water consumed and in activity and behavior are also important to note and could signal illness. Knowing your rabbit's regular routine is helpful in detecting when he is not feeling well.

For your pet's optimal care, it's important to choose a vet that specializes in rabbits.

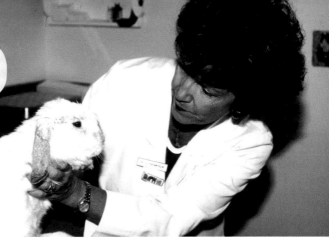

Any of these symptoms suggest that something might be wrong and a visit to the veterinarian is necessary.

Quite often, initial indications that a rabbit may be sick are subtle, and his facial expressions certainly won't give you any information as to his current state of well-being. Nevertheless, experienced rabbit owners and breeders can usually get to know their animals well enough to recognize these subtle changes. As you gain experience caring for your rabbit, especially if you develop a long-term interest, you will also become more proficient.

Unfortunately, rabbits do not usually show obvious signs of illness early in the course of a disease. The ability to hide an illness is believed to be a self-protective behavior because, in the wild, a weak or ill animal is easy prey for predators. By the time you realize that your rabbit is not well, he has usually been sick for quite some time. In many cases, treatment is difficult because the condition is more advanced at the time of detection. Although some diseases progress rapidly and an affected rabbit can die in 24 hours, early recognition may mean the difference between life and death for your pet. By familiarizing yourself with the symptoms of various ailments, you may be better prepared to recognize and better communicate his symptoms to your veterinarian.

Infectious Diseases

Infectious diseases are caused by bacteria, viruses, and protozoa. A rabbit with an infectious disease, as

Regular veterinary checkups help to prevent potential health problems.

Changes in your rabbit's appearance or behavior may signal he is ill.

determined by your veterinarian, should be isolated from any other animals to prevent it from spreading. These diseases can be passed from one rabbit to another in a variety of ways, including clothes, hands, and food bowls. Be sure to wash your hands, and do not share supplies and accessories between an infected rabbit and any others without first thoroughly disinfecting each item. Professional breeders are extra cautious and often use disposable surgical gloves when tending to sick rabbits.

Sometimes an infectious disease is subclinical, meaning signs of infection are difficult to detect. Individuals also differ in their resistance to infectious organisms. Some exposed rabbits never display any symptoms at all. However, stress or other bacterial or viral infections can cause a rabbit to suddenly become sick. A single rabbit is less at risk for infectious diseases compared to a rabbit kept in close proximity to large numbers of other rabbits. Environmental stress such as overcrowding, poor sanitation, malnutrition, and concurrent infection are predisposing factors to most diseases. Infectious diseases are often preventable through good husbandry.

Pasteurella

Pasteurella bacteria infection is the most common infectious disease of rabbits. The bacteria usually infect the upper respiratory tract, but can affect any

Quarantine your pet from other animals if he is diagnosed with an infectious disease.

part of the rabbit's body, causing ear infections, abscesses, and pneumonia. Pasteurellosis is often called snuffles because the most common symptoms are runny eyes, sneezing, coughing, and a thick discharge from the nose. The inside of the rabbit's front legs will be dirty from nose wiping.

A rabbit with these symptoms must be seen by a veterinarian. Pasteurellosis is diagnosed from cultures and blood tests. The symptoms are easy to treat, but the disease cannot be cured and is sometimes fatal. Antibiotics are used to treat mild cases of snuffles and can relieve a rabbit's symptoms. Injections are often preferred because many oral antibiotics cause additional problems.

Pasteurellosis is easily transmitted among rabbits by sneezing or close contact. Many rabbits are chronically infected, but only show signs of infection when stressed. A dirty cage, ammonia, and poor air circulation are some of the conditions that can cause a relapse.

Parasites

Parasites are organisms that survive by living and feeding on other organisms. When pet rabbits are obtained from a reputable source and kept in a clean environment, parasites are not a common problem for pet rabbits. Two of the most common types that affect them are fleas and ear mites.

Fleas

If the family dog or cat has fleas, then it is possible for your rabbit to become infested with them as well. Scratching is the most obvious symptom. You might also see the fleas or their dark droppings. A treatment approved for use on kittens is usually safe to use on your rabbit. However, your veterinarian might recommend one of the spot-on flea control products, which are more convenient. Besides treating your rabbit, you must also treat his cage

Signs of Emergency

The following symptoms indicate a rabbit needs immediate emergency care. Don't "wait to see what happens," or it could be too late.

bleeding
bloated abdomen
broken bones
constant teeth grinding
constipation
labored breathing
loss of appetite, refusal to eat
lying on side, will not get up
noticeable salivation
paralysis
rapid breathing
seizures
sitting hunched, reluctant to move
sudden weakness
tilted head
watery diarrhea

Zoonotic Diseases

Zoonotic diseases can be transmitted from animals to people. It is possible for humans to contract some ailments from rabbits, but it is not a frequent occurrence. Your veterinarian will be aware of such diseases, such as salmonella and ringworm, and can help you take preventive measures if your rabbit is diagnosed with one.

The potential for disease transmission is reduced with proper hygiene, such as washing your hands after playing with your rabbit or after cleaning his cage. Purchasing your pet from a clean environment rather than a smelly, dirty one also reduces the chance of him having a zoonotic disease.

Although not considered a zoonotic disease, some people are allergic to rabbits. The allergy can be to dander, hairs, and/or nail scratches. Should you develop symptoms such as a rash and sneezing, see your physician for further advice.

and surroundings. A flea comb can be used to help control and remove them in between treatments. Don't forget to also treat your dog and cat.

Hair Loss

Loss of hair can be caused by a variety of factors, including some parasites. Bald patches between the shoulder blades and down the back are often due to fur mites. Loss of hair on the feet, legs, and head can sometimes be due to ringworm, which is a fungus. Ringworm usually causes hair loss in round patches. The skin without hair is often red and may be covered

with a dry crust. Because ringworm is contagious to people, any rabbit with hair loss should be examined by a veterinarian who will provide an accurate diagnosis and treatment.

Most breeds of rabbit can remain quite healthy if they receive adequate daily care and attention.

Ear Mites

Ear mites live in a rabbit's ear canals and cause a dark crusty discharge. They also make his ears very itchy, causing him to scratch at them and shake his head constantly. The scratching can lead to infected wounds on or inside his ears. Your veterinarian must diagnose them using a microscope because they are not visible to the naked eye. Medication will eliminate the condition, but must be continued for several weeks to kill all stages of the mite's life cycle.

Noninfectious Ailments

Noninfectious diseases are not typically transmitted from one rabbit to another. The following are descriptions of some of the ailments that a rabbit can get.

Bladder Stones/Sludge

Bladder stones in rabbits are typically caused by a diet too high in calcium.

A rabbit's ears are the most sensitive part of his body.

Unlike people, who get rid of extra calcium in their stools, rabbits excrete it in their urine. The extra calcium can make the urine thick and pasty with whitish-tan calcium carbonate sediment. It can also form sludge or stones in the rabbit's bladder that make urination difficult and painful.

If you see your rabbit straining to urinate or hunched in pain, take him to your veterinarian. Stones can also affect the kidneys and other parts of the urinary tract.

If caught early enough, your veterinarian might be able to treat the

83

Antibiotics Caution

Infectious diseases that are caused by bacteria are treated with antibiotics. Rabbits are very sensitive to the effects of certain antibiotics such as penicillin. They can be harmful because they alter the useful bacteria that normally live in their digestive system (good bacteria or gut flora). A rabbit is not usually sensitive to the drug, as much as he is susceptible to the effects of it on the natural intestinal fauna. The wrong antibiotic can completely destroy the good bacteria, which can lead to the rabbit's death. Some allow harmful bacteria to grow by killing other naturally occurring types. These noxious bacteria produce toxins that can then kill a rabbit.

You don't need to worry about which antibiotics are appropriate for your rabbit. Your veterinarian will know what types can be safely used, as well as the recommended dosages for specific conditions.

Ear This

A rabbit's ears are the most sensitive area of his body. While mites, infections, wax accumulation, and other maladies in your rabbit's ears do not always represent an emergency, they do require immediate attention and treatment. Not doing so can put your pet's health in danger and can rapidly escalate to an emergency situation.

rusty red. The source of the color is not definitively known, but even wild rabbits make dark red urine. The red color is not an indication of blood in the urine, which usually must be detected under a microscope.

Hairballs/Gastric Stasis

Hair is common in the stomachs of healthy rabbits. They regularly shed their hair, some of which is swallowed when they groom themselves. Problems develop when it is not passed out of the rabbit's stomach, but accumulates into a hairball, which leads to the development of gastric stasis. Unlike cats, rabbits cannot vomit and throw up the hairballs. Loss of appetite and few or no droppings are the most common results of this problem. An affected rabbit might not eat for two to seven days. Any droppings he passes are smaller and fewer in number and may contain hair.

condition without surgery. Interestingly, many rabbits produce thick urine, but do not develop problems with bladder sludge or stones. Rabbits who have had sludge or a stone removed should be permanently switched from alfalfa-based to timothy-based pellets, which are lower in calcium. To encourage drinking enough water, some veterinarians also recommend that it be provided in a bowl, along with the usual sipper bottle method.

Red Urine

Normal rabbit urine is cloudy and can range in color from light yellow to

To ensure the best recovery, treatment should be sought at the first sign of illness.

Regular brushing is necessary to reduce the amount of loose hair your rabbit may swallow.

surgical removal of hairballs is sometimes required if the mass in the stomach is excessively dry. Because a rabbit that needs surgery is likely to be sicker, the chances of success are greatly reduced.

Hair is not the only cause of this condition. It can also occur when a rabbit is fed the wrong diet—one that is too high in carbohydrates and too low in fiber. Prevention includes feeding the right diet and regular brushing to reduce the amount of loose hair a rabbit might swallow. Some veterinarians suggest the preventative use of petroleum laxatives and offering juices that contain protein digesting enzymes, such as fresh pineapple or papaya juice in addition to feeding loose hay.

Gastric stasis means your rabbit's digestive system can no longer move food through it and it becomes "stuck." It is an emergency that requires immediate veterinary care. If left untreated, the rabbit will die. A veterinarian can usually palpate the stomach and locate a large, doughy mass. However, even a small hairball, which might not be readily detected, can be serious if it blocks the passage of the stomach's contents into the small intestine. He can diagnose hairballs with X rays, but doing so is not always definitive. The X rays might show a large mass in the rabbit's stomach or they may show the presence of gas in the stomach and intestines, which suggest gastric stasis.

The preferred method of treatment is re-hydration of the rabbit, which re-hydrates the stomach contents and stimulates gastric motility. Most rabbits respond to this treatment. However,

Keep It Clean!

A clean cage is one of the most important ways you can help your pet stay healthy. Spoiled food and a dirty cage are invitations to illness. Routine hygiene is the most effective way to prevent opportunistic and unhealthy organisms from becoming established in your rabbit's home and overpowering his natural resistance to disease. He is most likely to get sick when you become forgetful about maintaining his home environment.

Feeling Good

Care of a Sick Rabbit

Taking proper care of a sick rabbit can help his recovery. Keep your pet in a warm, quiet area and monitor his water and food intake, as well as his urine and fecal output. After any kind of surgery, make sure his cage remains clean to prevent any secondary bacterial infections at the surgery site. Check the incision each day for swelling or discharge. Also monitor if he is chewing the stitches. Be sure to consult with your veterinarian if your rabbit has not eaten within 24 hours after returning home.

Pudding Stools

Pudding stools are very soft, sticky droppings. They might stick to the cage or even to your rabbit's fur. Normal hard droppings do not smell, but pudding stools can reek. This condition is caused by a disruption in the normal microflora in the gastrointestinal tract. The ultimate cause can be a diet too high in protein, too high in carbohydrates (such as treats with grains as the main ingredient), or too low in fiber. The bacteria and protozoa in a rabbit's gut are very sensitive and easily thrown out of balance by the wrong foods or sudden changes in diet.

While pudding stools are not a serious condition, they do indicate that your rabbit is eating the wrong foods. If you don't change his diet, a more serious gastrointestinal disease, such as gastric stasis, could result. Pudding stools can be cured by feeding more hay, less pellets, and eliminating any treats other than small amounts of vegetables.

Lumps and Bumps

A lump under your rabbit's skin could be a tumor or an abscess. If you notice a swelling or bump, your pet needs to be seen by a veterinarian who can determine what it is. If it is a tumor and it is diagnosed to be cancerous, surgery might be necessary to remove the growth.

An abscess is caused by bacterial infection. If the lump is an abscess, your veterinarian will use a needle to biopsy (or sample) it, then drain and clean the site. Usually, a topical antibiotic is applied to the area. The bacteria that cause an abscess are often opportunistic

While recovering, keep your rabbit in a warm, quiet area, and handle him only when necessary.

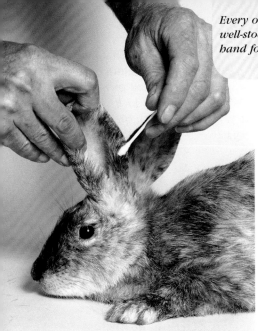

temperatures (above 85°F/29.4°C) for a long period of time, they can experience heatstroke. A rabbit that is stressed from heat will stretch out and breathe heavily. He might pant like a dog, which indicates a very serious situation. Once he is really dehydrated, he will stop panting and will be in serious danger. Therefore, long before he reaches this state, you must cool him down. Do not put him into cold water or use ice cubes as he could go into shock. Instead, wet his ears with a cool cloth, place a wet towel on him, and immediately get him to a veterinarian.

Rabbits do not necessarily drink more water when temperatures rise, and they might even drink less. Thus, shade and cool air temperatures are very important to prevent heatstroke.

and can infect other organs besides the skin. It is important that your rabbit be properly treated. Your veterinarian might need to culture a sample of the fluid to identify the type of bacteria present. An antibiotic selected on the basis of the culture and sensitivity test results is likely to be highly effective.

Also, because infection from bacteria is always possible when a rabbit is bitten in a fight, immediately clean any injuries with warm water and an antiseptic. Watch the wounds and if you detect any prolonged swelling, take him to your veterinarian. Swelling on the side of the face is often an abscess in the rabbit's cheek caused by malocclusion of molar teeth.

Heatstroke
Rabbits are very sensitive to heat. When they are exposed to high

Diarrhea Warning

As in small children, diarrhea can be fatal to your rabbit. There are different levels, the most visible being the runny form that has a strong odor. But a less obvious form is a pellet dropping that appears normal, but is sticky when you attempt to do a cleanup. Runny diarrhea requires an immediate trip to the vet. If your rabbit passes sticky stools or if they persist for more than two days, he should also be seen by a vet.

Feeling Good

A well-cared-for rabbit can live up to 15 years.

strong. If a rabbit is not securely held when picked up, he can kick violently with his powerful hind legs. Not only can the kicking result in fractures to the leg bones, but the vertebrae can fracture and damage the spinal cord. Also, because owners might be scratched by a struggling rabbit, they may sometimes drop him, causing further harm.

Properly holding your rabbit can prevent such injuries from occurring. Be extra cautious when placing him into his cage or onto the floor. This is when you are most likely to be scratched because he feels least secure and often begins to struggle. Returning your rabbit to his cage hind end first can prevent him from kicking.

Traumatic Injuries

Due to improper handling, rabbits are prone to traumatic injuries. Their skeletons are delicate and lightweight, but their muscles, which are developed for running, are extremely

Teeth Problems/Malocclusion

Rabbits sometimes need veterinary care due to malocclusion. For reasons due to heredity, trauma, infection, or an improper diet that does not include enough hard foods to wear them down, a rabbit's teeth can fail to meet and wear properly.

Maloccluded teeth can prevent a rabbit from eating. The animal will lose weight and can starve to death. He might show a symptom referred to as "slobbers," which are threads of saliva around the mouth that are sometimes wiped on the front paws. Another sign is droppings that contain large pieces of undigested food because the rabbit cannot chew properly.

Although a rabbit with malocclusion will show interest in food, he will not eat or food may drop from his mouth as he tries to chew because he is in pain. If you notice your rabbit is not eating, check his incisors by pulling back his lips. If they appear normal, but his symptoms persist for more than a day, you must take him to your veterinarian for an examination. Only he or she can diagnose malocclusion of the molars. Left untreated, misaligned molars can cut the rabbit's tongue and soft cheeks, resulting in an abscess.

Overgrown incisors are easily treated by a veterinarian. While the

Overheating

Rabbits do not deal very well with excessive heat. In their natural habitats, they live deep in burrows where temperatures remain cool and constant. Always be sure that your rabbit's cage is not in direct sunlight and that he has plenty of water and a cool place to retreat to. Never take him outdoors during the hottest part of the day as he could suffer from dehydration, or worse, heatstroke.

rabbit is still conscious, the vet can clip overgrown teeth. However, this procedure sometimes does not produce good long-term results and can cause other problems to develop. An incisor can split, fracture, or have jagged edges. If it splinters all the way to the gum, it not only will cause the rabbit pain, it might also allow bacteria to enter and form an abscess in the root. When clipped teeth are left with jagged edges, the inside of the rabbit's mouth and his

A rabbit that is in pain will sit still in a bunched up position for prolonged periods.

Lack of interest in food may be the result of a serious dental problem.

tongue might be cut by the rough edges, causing further discomfort and possible sites for infection.

Misery Loves Company

When your bunny is sick, do not separate him from his bonded partner unless the veterinarian feels it is necessary for him to be quarantined. In some cases, separating them can be detrimental in that it will cause undue stress and anxiety. If the problem is contagious, chances are that the cagemate was already exposed, so further exposure won't do more harm, but it's still a good idea to have both animals checked and treated by your vet. Also, you should separate the animals if one has had surgery as the cagemate may groom the treated site and try to chew out the stitches.

To prevent such problems, many veterinarians prefer to use a high-speed drill, which leaves a smooth surface while cutting through the overgrown incisors without splitting or fracturing them. The only potential drawback is that your rabbit must be sedated for this procedure. As an alternative to constantly trimming overgrown incisors, your veterinarian might discuss the possibility of extracting these teeth. However, because of their long roots, this process is sometimes difficult to successfully perform. Rabbits with overgrown molars must also be sedated. Specially designed cheek dilators and mouth specula help to open the rabbit's mouth so that molar teeth can be appropriately treated.

Senior Rabbits

As your rabbit gets older, you might begin to notice changes in his because they are less active. Overweight seniors have a harder time grooming themselves and can be more susceptible to skin problems. For a variety of reasons, they can have more problems with overgrown teeth, which can lead to difficulties in maintaining a healthy weight.

Your veterinarian can help manage all of these conditions for your senior pet. Providing the appropriate medical treatment can help prolong your rabbit's life. Seniors should have veterinary checkups once every six months to catch an illness or disease early, including blood tests and urinalysis. Starting a program of extended veterinary care, along with special home care, diet, and appropriate exercise can maintain his quality of life extremely well as he ages.

Look, Don't Touch

Although it is only natural that you would want to nurture and comfort an ailing pet, do not handle your rabbit more than usual while he is ill. Normally skittish, he is usually better off if left in peace to recuperate. This does not mean leaving him alone, but you can reassure him by talking softly to him, caressing him gently with some petting, or offering him treats if he's allowed to eat. Senior rabbits, especially, need to be handled more carefully as they will develop aches and pains from conditions due to aging, like arthritis.

behavior and body condition due to aging. Middle-aged and older rabbits are more prone to illnesses than when they were young. Once your rabbit is older than about six or seven years of age, he might experience stiffness and arthritis in his joints. In particular, rabbits can have problems with their back legs. Besides decreased activity due to age, older rabbits can become inactive due to joint pain. Some become overweight

Feeling

Frequent veterinary visits are recommended when your rabbit begins aging.

Chapter 6

Being Good

Training and proper handling can strengthen the bond between you and your rabbit. However, the first thing a pet should learn from his owner is that he can trust him or her to be consistent and patient while he settles in to his new home. Later on, providing a routine will make him feel secure and let him know what's expected of him. Although you can't train a rabbit to follow complex commands as a dog would, you can hand tame him, teach him some simple tricks, and share many fun activities together. This can be one of the most enjoyable parts of owning a rabbit, so be sure to make the process fun for both of you.

Training can strengthen the bond between you and your rabbit.

Hand Taming

You can start taming your rabbit by placing your hand in his cage and letting him get used to your smell, the sound of your voice, and being gently stroked along the cheeks or top of the head. Start taming your rabbit by visiting with him in the late afternoon or early morning, when he is most awake. Offer him a food treat from your hand. Place your hand with the treat inside your rabbit's cage. His curiosity will prompt him to investigate and eat the treat. Do not startle him by making sudden movements or loud noises. Once your rabbit is familiar with you and daily life in your home, such events are less likely to frighten him. When you pass your rabbit's cage, call his name and say hi. Once your rabbit knows you, he will run to the cage door to greet you, asking for attention. If you consistently work with your

rabbit, he will soon trust you and want to spend time with you.

Proper Handling

Proper handling is necessary to ensure that neither you nor your pet is unnecessarily hurt. It also helps your rabbit become accustomed to being held and petted, as well as teaching him that humans are friendly. In time, he may come to you on his own looking for some attention and snuggling.

To pick up your rabbit correctly, place one hand under his chest, just behind his front legs, then scoop your other hand under his rump. Immediately bring him against your stomach. Your rabbit will rest on your forearm. Your other hand should always remain on his shoulders to provide extra security. In some cases, he might kick a little. Smooth back his ears and tuck his head under your arm. With his head and eyes covered, he is more likely to remain quiet and relaxed while carried. It shouldn't need to be said, but never pick your rabbit up by his ears. Always support his hindquarters, and never let his hind legs dangle while you are carrying him. If he kicks, he can fracture or dislocate his spine.

It can take patience and practice for your rabbit to get used to being picked up and carried. You might want to wear long sleeves to protect your arms from possible scratches until he is more comfortable with the process.

Litter Box Training

Rabbits can be trained to use a litter box in their cages, or while they are out exercising in their playroom or exercise pen. However, they cannot be housetrained like a dog or cat. Rabbits are not as consistent. Teaching them to use a litter box can take time, from one week to a month or more.

Start the process by watching where your rabbit goes to the bathroom in his cage. He will probably establish an area in one corner, away from his nest box. After a few days, place a litter box containing some soiled bedding in this corner. Putting some hay in it will also encourage him to use the litter box. It is perfectly fine for him to sit there eating hay, as he will not consume the dirty portions.

While he is in his playroom or exercise pen, provide several litter boxes in various locations to housetrain your rabbit while he is

FAMILY-FRIENDLY TIP

Rabbits Are Not Toys

A child's age and maturity determine how much parental involvement is necessary in caring for and owning a pet. Generally, children younger than eight years of age must be taught how to treat an animal with care and respect. They must learn that it is not a toy and has needs separate from their own desires.

The rambunctious, uninhibited behavior of young children can frighten a rabbit. Hitting, shouting, poking, pulling his ears, running around screaming—all these behaviors can lead to a traumatized pet. With a parent's help, a child can learn how to be compassionate, how to play gently, and what hurting means. He can show a child how to sit quietly in the rabbit's play room or exercise pen, speak softly, move slowly, and gently pet him when he comes to visit.

Children, young ones in particular, sometimes unknowingly hurt an animal when trying to pick him up. Rough handling can frighten a rabbit and cause him to scratch or bite. A parent should reduce this risk by showing the child how to properly hold him. However, a parent must first consider whether the child is strong enough to pick up and hold the animal. In general, young children need to be watched when they are playing with their pets.

Being Good

out of his cage. He is likely to have fewer accidents if he has more options available to him. Each litter box should have sufficient litter, soiled bedding, and hay to attract him. Pay attention to your rabbit while he is wandering. When he crouches, extending his rear and tail, he is about to urinate. If he is in a litter box, praise him and give him a treat after he is done. If he is not, tell him no, and place him in his litter box. Do not scare or punish him, though, and do not make him frightened of you or the litter box. If he does urinate on the carpet, you must clean the spot with a product designed to completely remove pet odors or he is likely to use this spot again. (Keep in mind that spayed and neutered rabbits are more likely to consistently use a litter box and not mark with their urine.) Remember, it will take time and patience for your rabbit to become housetrained.

Exercise for House Rabbits

Time to play and exercise outside of the cage is essential for your rabbit. You should decide if you will let him have the run of one room or if you will have him exercise in a portable puppy pen. If your rabbit will be allowed to play in a room, you must "pet-proof" it before you let him loose.

Phone wires and exposed electrical cords must be placed out of reach. Some people put electrical cords in hard plastic piping to protect their pets from chewing them and electrocuting

themselves, or possibly starting a fire. Any items lying about, such as shoes, plants, or books on a low shelf, should be placed out of your rabbit's reach. They will also chew wooden furniture. Although it does not look attractive, you can put bubble wrap, which is sold at shipping stores, around the furniture legs. Bitter sprays sold in pet stores to discourage chewing are not usually effective.

Keep in mind that your rabbit will not just stay put on the floor, but can hop onto a couch, a chair, or a table. From there, he can access parts of the room that you thought were off-limits. To keep him in his play room, install temporary gates or close the door.

Handling your rabbit correctly ensures that neither you nor your rabbit are unnecessarily hurt.

Many people let their rabbits exercise while they are busy doing other things. However, even though the room is pet-proofed, you should know that they can cause damage. (Many owners are surprised and horrified at just how destructive one bunny can be!) They are natural gnawers and burrowers. They might dig at and chew the edges of carpet, urinate on rugs and furniture, scratch wood floors, chew floorboards, wood doors, wallpaper, or even sheetrock. They can squeeze into small spaces and get behind an area you did not want them to access. A rabbit can crawl under a couch or recliner, chew the furniture's underside, become stuck, or get injured if someone sits on him. Eating carpet or blanket fibers can also cause an expensive, potentially life-threatening digestive blockage that must be treated by your veterinarian.

Knowing about these potential hazards should not dissuade you from letting your rabbit exercise out of his cage. Rather, it means you must supervise him during play time. You cannot change his natural behavior, but you can plan for it, redirect it, monitor it, and keep both your pet and home safe.

Alternatively, you can use a portable puppy exercise pen set up in a given area. When not in use, the pen folds and can be easily stored away. Whether you use a pen or a pet-proofed room, provide your rabbit with toys so he has

The Expert Knows

Positive Reinforcement

Rabbits cannot be trained in the same way you train a dog, nor can you expect the same type of responsiveness. But you can apply the same approach, which relies on positive reinforcement. Using a small tidbit of food or praise, you can encourage desirable behaviors. When your rabbit is doing something good, reward him. When he is doing something bad, correct him. Firmly say "no," clap your hands to get his attention, or remove him from the area so he cannot continue his bad behavior. No matter what, do not hit your rabbit. He will not understand, and you are likely to scare him and destroy his trust in you.

something to do. You can include cardboard boxes, tunnels, and paper bags. Place hay into an empty cereal box and make him work to get it out.

Building Trust

Supervising your pet shouldn't be work, but, instead, the fun time you get to play and visit with him. You should begin by letting your rabbit explore from his cage. Place it on the floor or build a ramp so he can easily get in and out of it. Your rabbit will use the cage as a familiar home base. Open the door and invite him to come out by calling his name. It might take awhile, but his curiosity will eventually cause him to hop out.

You can assist your rabbit when he is first learning about his playroom or

Rabbits

*Exercise and play time out-
side of the cage is essential to
your rabbit's mental and
physical well-being.*

in which he likes to play. Be careful that he does not chew anything when he is roaming. Your rabbit might find an item he wants, grab it, and run away with it to chew in peace. If you hear or see him do something you don't want him to do, firmly say "no!" If your pet persists, try clapping your hands at the same time to get his attention so he will stop.

Once your rabbit knows his playroom well, you will find that he seeks you out for attention. Try calling him to you and rewarding him with a small treat. You can also teach him to stand on his hind legs to get a treat, or toss a small ball for him to chase in a game of catch. For a different, more quiet kind of bonding time, you can brush him.

Don't forget to provide one or more litter boxes in exercise areas. Be prepared to move the location of the boxes to wherever your rabbit seems to prefer.

pen. Your objective is to build his confidence and avoid having him become frightened. Sit quietly, don't make any sudden movements, and talk quietly to him. Encourage your rabbit to return to his home base frequently by restricting his first explorations to a small area. Block off other parts of the room using furniture or cardboard boxes. You don't want him to be able to dart away, become frightened, or difficult to return to his cage. Gradually increase the size of the area your rabbit can explore.

Eventually, your rabbit will know the entire room and will be very confident when out exploring. You will discover that he has favorite areas

Be Patient!

It is important to be patient and aware that what you perceive as bad behavior is generally what comes naturally to your rabbit, and, in some cases, is just a defense mechanism. In his natural world, everything larger is a predator to be feared and avoided. Therefore, you need to understand these behaviors and establish trust before beginning training, whether you are trying to solve a problem behavior or just engaging in a fun activity. Always be consistent as variations from routine will confuse your pet. Never punish him or yell at him, as he will not understand this and will likely just want to flee from you. In time, he'll become comfortable and will respond accordingly.

Outdoor Exercise

During nice weather, you can let your indoor house rabbit, or your outdoor rabbit, exercise in a protected area within your backyard. Use a grazing ark, puppy exercise pen, or construct a rabbit run with a permanent fence that extends more than one foot below the soil to prevent him from tunneling out. The fence should also be high enough to keep out dogs, cats, or other animals. Whatever enclosure you choose, it will need to include a sheltered area and fresh water. It is always best to be around to make sure your rabbit is safe while he is outside. In other words, don't leave to go shopping for several hours unless you are absolutely positive he is safe and secure and protected from hot or cold weather.

You can build your rabbit's trust by encouraging him with a healthy treat.

Keep It Simple

Rabbits aren't big on performing tricks. They are not acrobatic like rats or ferrets, and they did not evolve wanting to please people the way dogs do. Most of what you can teach a rabbit isn't clever, but can be useful. Not all will respond, but some can be taught simple commands such as coming when called, sitting up on their hind legs, or going into their cage when commanded.

You must be consistent and not give up. Some learn slower than others, and some trainers aren't as good as others. All these tricks rely on a small piece of tasty food to reward your pet when he performs correctly. For example, while sitting on the floor with your rabbit just a few feet away from you, call his name and say "come." Let him see and, hopefully, smell the treat so he comes to get it. Once he performs the command, you can increase the distance between you. It can be fun to think of your own tricks, too.

Walking and Leashes

While you can't walk your rabbit on a leash like you would a dog, you can follow around behind him and guide his exploration. Essentially, your rabbit will take you for a walk, while you keep him away from any hazards. Use a figure-H or a figure-8 harness, along with a lightweight leash no longer than 6 feet (1.8 m). Longer ones can get tangled and allow your rabbit to get beyond a safe distance. The leash should attach to the girth portion of the harness, not to the collar.

Let your rabbit get used to wearing his harness for a few days before you attach the leash. Do not pull or yank him. Walking him outside your backyard is not recommended. There are many potential hazards that could frighten him, including loose dogs and backfiring cars.

Problem Behaviors

Young rabbits are playful, curious, and energetic. When they reach sexual maturity, they can become ornery due to their raging hormones. Your rabbit will probably be more independent and less cuddly. Spaying or neutering can help reduce some of the more obnoxious behaviors (see Chapter 1). However, just as young dogs have lots of energy, so, too, will your young bunny. He will calm down after a year or so. Unfortunately, due to an unwillingness to deal with their rabbits' high energy, many people get rid of their pets right before this stage ends. Senior rabbits are mellow, slow down, sleep more, and are less likely to be destructive.

Besides the behaviors already discussed, such as chewing, some pet owners have problems with their rabbits nipping or biting. There are

Your rabbit displays a variety of behaviors in response to different stimuli. Recognizing and understanding his body language and behavior will help you to tame and train him.

biting – dominance; angry; fearful; warning (go away now)

charging – pay attention to me; warning (go away)

chewing – keeping teeth trim

chin rubbing – territorial scent marking

circling feet – courtship; sexual behavior

digging – natural behavior

ears back – warning (leave me alone); might bite

ears forward – alert; curious

freezing low to ground – frightened; trying to hide

grunts – angry; might bite

happy bunny dance – kicking up heels, jumping, twisting in mid air, racing around, leaping on and off furniture

head shake – annoyed

loud continual teeth grinding – in pain

lunging – warning (go away); scared; angry

lying on ground, legs sprawled behind – very relaxed

nipping – warning (leave me alone)

nudging – pet me; feed me

scattered droppings – marking territory

scream – badly hurt

sitting up – curious

spraying urine – marking territory

teeth grinding, chuckling – contented

thumping hind legs – scared; angry

tongue kisses – showing affection by grooming you

tossing objects – playing

Never punish a rabbit for "bad behavior," like chewing; he is only doing what comes naturally to him.

several potential reasons for this, including fear or guarding territory. Those that bite from fear will usually stop when whatever scared them is eliminated. A more difficult case to correct is when a rabbit becomes territorial in his cage and nips whenever you put your hand inside, even when you are giving him his food. Squawking in pain might help, as can gently holding your rabbit's head to the cage floor for a few seconds to assert your dominance. Hand feeding him some tasty treats outside his cage will help him associate your hand with the arrival of goodies. Place the treat on your flat open hand, and make your rabbit come toward you to get it. Once he routinely eats from your hand, you can offer him the treat while your hand is next to the cage, and finally while your hand is inside his cage.

Introducing Two Rabbits

Rabbits are social animals with dominance hierarchies. They are also territorial. These behaviors can lead to some impressive fights should you decide to get a second rabbit, but do not properly introduce him to your original pet. Even littermates or two different rabbits that grew up together might fight once they reach sexual maturity. Two females are just as likely to scrap as are two males. Spaying or neutering can reduce the likelihood of fights occurring. A female and male will get along, but should be altered so they will not constantly have young.

You must introduce a new rabbit in neutral territory that neither has ever visited. Using a small room such as the bathroom can work. It is positive if the two rabbits ignore each other or rest quietly. Aggressive ones will put their ears back, growl, and box each other with their front feet. If their interaction escalates to chasing and biting with fur flying, you must separate them. Use a towel or squirt gun so you won't get bitten or scratched.

You can also try placing each rabbit in his own cage, and setting the cages side by side. Keep this arrangement awhile and see if their aggression fades. It can take patience

Initial Introductions

When introducing your new rabbit to other rabbits be sure to do so in neutral territory, as they tend to be rather territorial creatures. Continue introductions over several days under close supervision until you see that all parties are getting along well together. Don't try to rush or expect instant success. As with humans, relationships take time to grow. Even if you feel your animals have adjusted and accept one another, it's a good idea to always supervise interactions with other pets such as cats and dogs.

and persistence to get two rabbits to like each other. Once they do, though, you will enjoy watching them groom,

Before you can train rabbits, you need to understand their behavior.

Being Good

Introduce your new rabbit to established pets gradually to avoid territorial disputes.

play, and sleep together. Not all rabbits will bond. It is best if you acquire the second rabbit on a trial basis so he can be returned if the situation does not work out.

Introducing a Dog or Cat

It is possible for some dogs and cats to befriend a house rabbit, which can certainly make your household run more smoothly. However, it is not necessary. At the least, you want your other pets trained to tolerate your rabbit without chasing or harassing him. If you constantly have to worry about his safety, it will be very stressful.

Ideally, your dog knows basic obedience commands such as sit, stay, and lie down, and you are capable of controlling him. Let the animals first meet while your rabbit is still in his cage. Correct your dog if he barks, paws at the cage, jumps around, or otherwise scares him. Once he is used to the rabbit in his cage, he is ready to meet him outside of it. Have your dog on a leash and make him lie down while your rabbit is exploring. Do not let him lunge or bark at the rabbit. Reward him with praise or a food treat for good behavior. Eventually, your rabbit's curiosity will cause him to approach and investigate your dog. Keep your canine under control and you are on your way toward encouraging their friendship. It is often best to perform out-of-cage introductions after your pooch has burned off energy on a long run.

Cats and rabbits can become friends, but be cautious with dwarfs and small breeds, as some cats are capable of hurting them. Medium and large breeds are usually able to discourage a cat and might even bound after them, scaring them away. For the introductions, either have your cat on a harness and leash or have a squirt gun handy. Correct undesirable behavior immediately, such as your cat whacking at your rabbit with his paw. Encourage suitable interactions with praise and a food treat. Even if your dog and cat become friendly with your rabbit, always supervise their interactions. As instincts can sometimes get the upper hand, never leave your rabbit alone with any natural predator at any time—even if it is a pet cat or dog!

It's generally not a good idea to allow your rabbit to interact with natural predators, like dogs and cats.

Resources

Clubs and Societies

American Rabbit Breeders Association, Inc. (ARBA)
P.O. Box 426
Bloomington, IL 61702
Phone: (309) 664-7500
Fax: (309) 664-0941
E-mail: ARBAPOST@aol.com
http://www.arba.net/

American Cavy Breeders Association
Secretary: Lenore Gergen
E-mail: McCavy@aol.com
http://www.acbaonline.com

American Federation of New Zealand Rabbit Breeders, Inc.
Secretary: Sam Rizzo
E-mail: Srizzo124@aol.com
http://www.geocities.com/newzealandrba/

The British Rabbit Council
Purefoy House, 7 Kirkgate
Newark, Notts, NG24 1AD
UK
Phone: 44 01636-676042
E-mail: info@thebrc.org
http://www.thebrc.org/

Internet Resources

Healthypet
http://www.healthypet.com
Healthypet.com is part of the American Animal Hospital Association, an organization of more than 29,000 veterinary care providers committed to providing excellence in small animal care.
Pets 911
http://www.1888pets911.org

Pets 911offers a comprehensive database of lost and found pets, adoption information, pet health, and shelter and rescue information.

The Small Animal Pages
http://www.pet-net.net/small_animals/rabbits.htm

This website provides pet information, chat groups, humor pages, and links to rescue groups and numerous other rabbit-related websites.

VetQuest
http://www.vin.com/vetquest/index0.html
VetQuest is an online veterinary search and referral service. You can search its database for over 25,000 veterinary hospitals and clinics all over the world.

Veterinary and Health Resources

American College of Veterinary Internal Medicine (ACVIM)
1997 Wadsworth Blvd., Suite A
Lakewood, CO 80214-5293
Telephone: (800) 245-9081
Fax: (303) 231-0880
Email: ACVIM@ACVIM.org

www.acvim.org

American Holistic Veterinary Medical Association (AHVMA)
2218 Old Emmorton Road
Bel Air, MD 21015
E-mail: office@ahvma.org
http://www.ahvma.org/

American Veterinary Medical
Association (AVMA)
1931 North Meacham Road-Suite 100

Schaumburg, IL 60173
E-mail: avmainfo@avma.org
http://www.avma.org

Animal Behavior Society
Indiana University
2611 East 10th Street #170
Bloomington IN   47408-2603

Telephone: (812) 856-5541
E-mail: aboffice@indiana.edu
www.animalbehavior.org

ASPCA Animal Poison Control Center
1717 South Philo Road, Suite 36
Urbana, IL 61802
Telephone: (888) 426-4435
www.aspca.org

British Veterinary Association (BVA)
7 Mansfield Street
London
W1G 9NQ
Telephone: 020 7636 6541
Fax: 020 7436 2970
E-mail: bvahq@bva.co.uk
www.bva.co.uk

Orthopedic Foundation
for Animals (OFA)

2300 NE Nifong Blvd
Columbus, Missouri 65201-3856
Telephone: (573) 442-0418
Fax: (573) 875-5073
Email: ofa@offa.org
www.offa.org

Rescue and Adoption Organizations

American Humane
Association (AHA)
63 Inverness Drive East
Englewood, CO 80112
Telephone: (303) 792-9900
Fax: 792-5333
www.americanhumane.org

American Society for
the Prevention of Cruelty to Animals
(ASPCA)

424 E. 92nd Street
New York, NY 10128-6804
Phone: (212) 876-7700
http://www.aspca.org

Best Friends
Animal Sanctuary

5001 Angel Canyon Road
Kanab, UT 84741-5001
Phone: (435) 644-2001
E-mail: info@bestfriends.org
http://www.bestfriends.com/

Friends of Rabbits
P.O. Box 1112
Alexandria, VA 22313
E-mail: information@friendsofrabbits.org
http://www.friendsofrabbits.org

House Rabbit Society
148 Broadway
Richmond, CA 94804
Phone: (510) 970-7575
E-mail: care@rabbit.org
http://www.rabbit.org/

Rabbit Welfare Association
RWF P.O. Box 603
Horsham, West Sussex RH13 5WL
England
Phone: 44 08700 465249
http://www.houserabbit.co.uk/

Royal Society for the Prevention of
Cruelty to Animals (RSPCA)
Telephone: 0870 3335 999
Fax: 0870 7530 284
www.rspca.org.uk

The Blue Cross
Shilton Road
Burford
Oxon OX18 4PF
England
Phone: 44 01993 825500
E-mail: info@bluecross.org.uk
http://www.bluecross.org.uk/

The Humane Society of the United
States (HSUS)
2100 L Street, NW
Washington DC 20037
Phone: (202) 452-1100
http://www.hsus.org

Publications

Magazines

Best Friends Magazine
5001 Angel Canyon Road
Kanab, UT 84741
http://www.bestfriends.com/news/
newshome.htm

Friends of Rabbits
Online Newsletter Archive
P.O. Box 1112
Alexandria, VA 22313
E-mail: information@friendsofrabbits.org
http://www.friendsofrabbits.org/
newsletters/newsletter.htm

House Rabbit Journal
148 Broadway
Richmond, CA 94804
http://www.psg.lcs.mit.edu/~carl/paige/
HRJ-articles.html

Rabbits Only Magazine
P.O. Box 207
Holbrook, NY 11741
E-mail: Danielle@overtureusa.com
http://www.rabbits.com/

The Rabbit Warren Magazine
E81B Daniels Road
Shelton, WA 98584
E-mail: RabbitWarrenMagazine@yahoo.com
http://therabbitwarren.tripod.com/

Index

109

Index

About the Author:

Sue Fox is the author of numerous books on small animals and several breeds of dog. Her home in the Sierra Nevada Mountains of California is shared with a happy menagerie.

Photo Credits:

Joan Balzarini: 45, 64, 79, 80
Bruce Cook: 11, 34, 43
Michael Gilroy: 19, 22, 26, 61, 74, 98, 103
Peter J. Land: 105
Horst Mayer: 9, 50, 60
Robert Pearcy: 76, 88
Vincent Serbin: 21, 42, 104
John Tyson: 35, 36, 38, 73, 84
Susan Webb: 102
All other photographs courtesy Isabelle Francais
Cover photo: Ng Yin Chern (Shutterstock)